HITLER'S ENGLISH GIRLFRIEND

HITLER'S ENGLISH GIRLFRIEND

GIRLFRIEND

THE STORY OF UNITY MITFORD

DAVID REHAK

AMBERLEY

*Dedicated to the victims of the Holocaust
and all other Nazi atrocities.*

This edition first published 2012

Amberley Publishing
The Hill, Stroud
Gloucestershire, GL5 4EP

www.amberley-books.com

British Library Cataloguing in Publication Data.
A catalogue record for this book is available from the British Library.

ISBN 978 1 4456 0845 7

Typesetting and Origination by Amberley Publishing.

Printed and bound in Great Britain by
Marston Book Services Ltd, Oxfordshire

For M. M.

Contents

Acknowledgements

This account was initially going to be about Irma Grese, who was the youngest high-ranking female Nazi to be tried and executed for war crimes, but after watching the 2007 BBC documentary *Hitler's British Girl*, I decided that Unity Mitford would provide even better material for the kind of book I wanted to write. So it was thanks to this intriguing TV documentary that I had the idea for this book.

First and foremost, before I began with my research and put a single word to paper, I thought it only fitting to visit the concentration camps of Auschwitz-Birkenau. The experience of it is like nothing you can get from a history book. To see how racial hatred can lead to people being treated worse than animals with one's own eyes – to the point where they are systematically exterminated and their body parts reused, i.e. hair in mattresses and skin turned into lampshades – is something I cannot, will not, ever forget. My conscience was so deeply shaken and saddened that a peculiar dark and heavy feeling haunted and consumed my soul for over a week after the visit.

I read many books full of reliable information to get a strong feel for my subject in preparation for writing this fact-based story. The abundance of research on the real Unity contained in David Pryce-Jones' 1976 study *Unity Mitford: A Quest* proved most helpful, especially in helping to corroborate evidence later found elsewhere, including things that Unity did and said. A French book about the Mitford sisters, *Les extravagantes soeurs Mitford* by

Emile Guicovaty, was also an eye-opening and informative read. Other titles I consulted include *The Mitfords: Letters between Six Sisters* by Charlotte Mosley; *Hons and Rebels* by Jessica Mitford; *Diana Mosley: Mitford Beauty, British Fascist, Hitler's Angel* by Anne de Courcy; *The House of Mitford* by Jonathan and Catherine Guinness; and *The Sisters: The Saga of the Mitford Family* by Mary S. Lovell. The 2009 BBC documentary *Wartime London with Harry Harris* also gave me much food for thought.

In addition, my book relies heavily on countless notes taken from interviews with around fifty people – descendants of those who knew Unity when she was growing up or as an adult – and several personal letters they kindly provided. Also, I extracted plenty of information from newspaper articles and unpublished documents, including official certificates, wartime files, etc. culled from dusty library archives from London, Prague, Munich and Berlin. Living in Central Europe as I do (the Czech Republic), it wasn't too expensive to catch a few relatively cheap flights (thank you Ryanair) or train rides to these places. I am indebted to the Prague City Archives, the German National Library, The Bavarian State Library, The London Metropolitan Archives, and the British Library's newspaper library. The National Archives in Britain were also particularly useful to my searches for new data, some of it newly declassified.

I knew immediately what I wanted to accomplish. This would be a work of narrative non-fiction, written in an entertaining, novelistic style. Simply put, in episodic, biographical narrative sequences, I wanted to recount all the poignant things Unity had ever done or said that were likely to chill or intrigue readers or have some other strong impression on them. I also wanted to include what her likely thoughts, feelings and motivations were, based on the evidence of her words and actions. Perhaps most importantly, I wanted to retell the true story of her intimate connection to Adolf Hitler, whom she met at least 140 times in a span of no less than five years in the crucial period leading up to the Second World War, and with whom she formed a close personal attachment.

She tried to seduce him in spite of their friendship, dreamed of becoming his wife, became his political puppet, and even tried to inspire a peace agreement between Britain and Germany to avoid the war. This is a unique and intriguing historical story, therefore it must be freshly examined in the light of our updated knowledge of it. And that is why it becomes the main focus of this book. I recount the most interesting factual aspects and incidents of the extraordinary and unprecedented close relationship between one misguided English girl and *the* Adolf Hitler, who has come to be known in the annals of history as the most notorious mass murderer of modern times, probably of all time. Why would a pretty young girl like Unity develop an obsession with this man? That is the question that I have tried to answer as clearly and engagingly as possible.

In order to accomplish this with success, it was necessary to painstakingly research the person and personality of Unity until I felt I knew her as well as anyone I have come to know personally. I read every recorded word that had ever come from her mouth and learned of all the significant and even insignificant moments in her life. The remembrances of those who really did know her greatly added to my understanding. After this task was completed, my other task was to obtain the true details of Unity's relationship with Hitler. I put together information new and old in order to narrate these extraordinary details in a digestible manner for the twenty-first century reader. This book is intended to be the first to thoroughly examine this curious relationship in a comprehensive way, taking into account more than seventy-five years of research, some of it hidden or hushed-up until quite recently. At last, this remarkable tale can be fully told.

I would like to thank everyone at Amberley for their hard work on this book project: the editors and designers.

'The Devil gets more help from fanatics than fools.'
—Sam Chadwick

THE REBEL WITHOUT A CAUSE

She entered into the open arms of the world on that dark and stormy day, 8 August 1914. The First World War had just broken out and her parents had been hoping for an alliance between Britain and Germany (her mother also adored an actress named Unity Moore), so they named their new baby daughter Unity. But now there was a deep divide between the two countries and the battle cries were blaring. The baby was given the middle name Valkyrie in honour of the war maidens in Wagner's famous opera, of which her father was fond.

She was born into one of the great aristocratic families of England. The Mitfords could trace their ancestors back almost a thousand years, to the Norman Conquest of 1066.

From the very start, baby Unity was a troublemaker, a real handful in more ways than one. But she was daddy's favourite, and he was a softie; mother was the disciplinarian.

Watching his little Unity, Lord Redesdale had such a gleam in his eye. He was bewitched by his mischievous little angel. Always. No matter what she did, he couldn't help it. All he could do was spoil her. If she behaved, he flooded her with praise or kisses; if she misbehaved, he ignored it.

Baby Unity loved putting things (any things) in her mouth. Just as long as it fit.

When she was two and a walking toddler, she walked (or wobbled) up to a table in the front hall, on which sat some very important keys, including those to the front door. Of course, she knew (or cared) nothing for this fact. She felt her baby teeth growing, and she liked to try them out on objects, especially inedible objects, so she began trying her tiny new teeth out on the keys. Besides, the metal from the keys had a nice and interesting taste. Needless to say that she had no conception of this 'taste test' being bad for her health, not to mention the risk of swallowing the keys and choking.

After nine years, little Unity was as pretty and incorrigible as ever. Few governesses could tolerate her for very long – few could stand up to her unrelentingly naughty misbehaviour. Unlike most children, Unity didn't seem to know fear, and would never learn that certain things were out of bounds.

Her pet-name was Bobo, and everybody called her that.

She had several sisters, but the one closest to her in age, whom she got on with the best in early childhood, was Jessica. Of course, Unity being Unity, they had their fair share of fights and disagreements as well, as all siblings are liable to have.

The Mitfords lived in a huge and imposing stone country mansion called Asthall Manor, next to the church graveyard. There were also a number of farms around the place.

Jessica and Unity, two little girls in puberty, strolling, running, and dancing among the churchyard tombs – picture it.

'When I die,' said Unity, 'I want to be buried standing up, not lying down.' She meant that she wanted her coffin to be interred vertically, not horizontally.

'That's daft!' said Jessica. 'I've never heard of such a silly thing. You can't be buried like that, because you can't stand up anymore when you're dead, you half-wit.'

A farmer came around the corner of the church, carrying a cute baby lamb folded in his arms.

'She's lovely!' exclaimed Jessica.

The farmer smiled. 'I'll let you have her if you like,' he said.

'Oh will you? Oh that's grand! Thank you, thank you!'

'Her name's Miranda,' said the farmer.

Unity stared on with envious eyes. *Why should she get it and not me?* she thought to herself. Her eyes were normally a sparkling bright blue, but yes, that moment they were tinted green with envy.

The very next day, Unity fell at her father's feet in the sitting room as he was reading the newspaper, astonishing him with the plea, 'Oh papa, I want a goat! Please let me have it, oh please do let me have it!'

She promptly got one.

She didn't want to imitate her sister and get a lamb, so she had opted for the goat instead. Perhaps in a way it was a sign of her rebelliousness, since goats are often thought of as a symbol of the Devil, while the lamb symbolises Jesus Christ. From that moment on, the two sisters argued over which one of them had the better pet.

Three years later, twelve-year-old Unity began insisting on dance lessons.

'I must learn to dance, I'm almost a teen!' exclaimed the precocious Unity. 'I'm not a little girl anymore...'

'You're not a little too young for it, my dear?' inquired her father innocently, gently patting her on the head.

'No!' was her firm and curt response. Then, more nicely: 'Papa, I'm not a baby anymore. I hate being treated like a doll. I want to do what I want! I have rights.'

Her sweet, benevolent papa raised his eyebrows and executed a weak half-chuckle. He gave in to her request: 'If you want to dance, then you shall dance!'

She embraced him tightly around the neck and sighed aloud with joy. Bobo was already interested in boys from an early age; dancing would give permission for close contact.

The lessons began.

Throughout the whole of her first waltz, Bobo's face beamed in a smile as she gazed into a freckle-faced redhead's eyes and occasionally let a few giggles slip as he led her, somewhat awkwardly at times, around the dance floor. It didn't matter to her that he wasn't necessarily the handsomest boy in the room – the important thing was the dance, the romance! She felt so grown-up.

Riding horses also appealed to her unfettered nature from this early age; she felt so fast and free on the back of her steed. No parental surveillance and supervision, just her and the breeze and the open countryside of her father's spacious estate. Speed gave her a great feeling. *Now it's a horse, later it will be a car*, she thought. She revelled in the refreshing exhilaration of adrenalin.

All that riding and other athletic exertion could, of course, work up an appetite. Bobo was a big girl, but not what one would call fat. Her favourite treat was whipped-cream walnuts, and she had a real talent for being able to swallow large amounts of cream and potatoes. She also loved milk and chocolate, together.

Unity was the last one to the dinner table. That didn't please her mother, as the family had to wait for a minute or so before starting dinner.

'Oh I do wish you wouldn't be so tardy!' exclaimed her mother – with whom she never got along and whom she seldom obeyed.

'I was out riding and lost track of the time,' Bobo sighed nonchalantly.

Lady Redesdale momentarily and motionlessly gave her daughter an evil, annoyed look, before feverishly starting to devour her meal, almost in a frenzy of hunger.

Unity didn't even pick up her utensil at first. Just sat there placidly as everyone started to eat. Then, she just started grimacing at her mother in a certain glaring way while really quickly and methodically stuffing her face with her mashed potatoes in mocking imitation of her mother, her gaze set in a grim and austere expression.

Her mother couldn't help but notice. She returned the stare; it was a game of who would out-stare whom.

But Bobo prevailed. Her mother smashed her fist down beside her plate and hissed: 'Stop doing that, damn you! Don't look at me like that!' Lady Redesdale was enraged.

Bobo gave out a half-subdued smirk. Smug in her little victory, she started eating normally and paid no more attention to her mother.

Lord Redesdale said nothing besides exclaim to his wife after sampling the dessert, 'My dear, you really must try this cranberry sauce. It's a Canadian concoction. Quite sour, but when sweetened with sugar, it's quite good; yes, really very good!'

Unity entered her teenage years with a desire to make herself stand out in some way in a family full of gifted siblings. From an early age she showed a knack for 'scribbling' – that is, drawing. She was the second youngest of six sisters, and most of them had a gift for a different kind of 'scribbling' – writing. But she was the one who could draw. She would always wish that she could write as they did, but she had no literary talent. She was much better as a reader than a writer.

She sat in bed wishing she had a lot of great books. Why didn't she own a copy of *The Oxford Book of English Verse*? It peeved her that she had read a fascinating book review of it in the newspaper but that she didn't have it.

She sat up and hopped over to the wall, removed a painting of some long-dead ancestor who meant nothing to her, and laid it down carelessly. *This is where my bookshelves will go*, she thought to herself. Indeed, in time she would accumulate a vast library and count Huxley and Waugh among her contemporary favourites. She was also a mad Brontë fan, and was fond of the dark, weird, mystical and fantastical, like William Blake or Edgar Allan Poe.

When she wasn't reading books, Unity was looking at pictures in them. Bobo glanced over at her writing table and picked up a different kind of book, opening it at random. She started pouring over the illustrated pictures of nudes by Renoir and other great artists. She felt entranced; felt herself moved by the enticing beauty of the female form. *Who were these women? And what were their lives like? Did they sleep with the painter after he painted them?*

Another great love was singing. Bobo was fond of whistling, and she could do it in tune – popular tunes of the day, hymns, whatever.

Unity threw the illustrated book of nudes on her bed. She decided she would look through the pictures again at bedtime. She would take the book to bed with her.

On impulse she suddenly ran down the flights of stairs, making a ruckus with her shoes on the hardwood landing. All the while, she pranced and whistled 'Oh God Our Help in Ages Past'. She didn't care for the words, she just liked the melody.

Stumbling into the dining hall, she realised that a dinner party was under way. Everyone became silent and turned to face the whistling girl. Lady Redesdale had a look of extreme annoyance and embarrassment and gave her daughter a look that could murder. Time froze for a moment and no one seemed to dare to move or even whisper. Unity snickered aloud, and then turned back into the hallway again, prancing along as before and whistling all the louder.

Jessica was only a year older than Unity. They became inseparable. They even invented a complete new language, which they named Boudledidge, or just Boud (pronounced 'Bowed'). It was impossible for anyone to understand it except for the two of them.

Unity and Jessica loved to gang up on whomever they chose as their next victim, referring to it as their 'sport', as in 'making sport of' so-and-so. One of them would say 'Boud', and that was the signal they exchanged before they would 'Boudledidgize' someone.

Unity, being Unity, 'translated' a number of dirty songs into Boud, so that she could sing them without repercussion in front of the adults. She sang away in the sitting room by the crackling fire while her father sat reading his evening paper a few feet away. He grinned at the nonsensical-sounding words, but Lady Redesdale, who was also in the room, stood up and marched out in an irritated huff. If only she had also known the dirty meaning of the words – one expects that she would have been twice as angry.

Asthall Manor, Unity's childhood home out in the country, was a grand and stately albeit isolated mansion and Unity sometimes felt the loneliness and rural seclusion of the place weigh heavily on her teenage soul. It made her feel rebellious and suffocated, made her want to get her kicks somehow by breaking the rules. With no close friends nearby, Unity invented an 'imaginary friend'. This 'friend' would have a bad influence on her and induce her to do bad things. She felt that this way she would have an excuse for her bad behaviour – she could place the blame elsewhere and not be responsible. The name of this made-up friend was Nasty Lady.

'Nasty Lady is guilty of all my naughtiness!' Bobo would say. 'I have no control over her whatsoever…'

So it was Nasty Lady who instructed Unity to do what was not allowed: to steal strawberries from the neighbor's fields or to eat chocolate at midnight when she should have been asleep hours ago. Likewise, it was Nasty Lady and not Unity who took Jessica's beloved stuffed teddies and stuck them full of pins.

Jessica had had enough. 'If you do that again,' she exclaimed, 'I won't be responsible for *my* actions either!'

'You know,' whispered Unity, kissing her sister on the cheek and pulling one of the pins out and pointing it at Jessica as if threatening to prick her with it, 'I usually adore you, but sometimes I can't stand you.'

Unity turned around to look out the bedroom window, deep in thought. Then and there, while gazing upon the beautiful blue expanse of the horizon, the conviction gripped her that she would not try to be friendly or charming to people she didn't like. People had to like her as she was or not at all. If they approved, well and good, but if not, they had only to reject her, as she would reject them. This pose of defiance pressed her down into a teenage gloom. When later extended into adult relationships, it could be very damaging. She was impervious to everyone else's feelings. *I will never let anyone hurt me or see me cry*, she thought to herself. *But to people I like, I shall be brilliant and charming. What is more, I have a wonderful shiny skin, almost transparent. Who cares that I also have a loud and defiant voice?*

Not surprisingly, it wasn't long after that Unity cornered her father in his study and blurted out the words: 'I'm bored of home. I want to go to boarding school at St Margaret's Bushey.' St Margaret's, better known as 'SMB' to its pupils, was one of those terribly posh, pretentious and prestigious girls' private schools full of the daughters of aristocrats and wealthy businessmen.

Her father paused for a moment, and then asked, very simply, 'Why do you want to go there?'

Bobo also paused. A much longer pause. Could she divulge that she longed to go there to gain ample room for wickedness?

'Fresh fields to conquer,' she retorted.

Her father looked at her dubiously. 'You would be on your own. And no privacy. Just dormitories full of silly girls. It's a strict school, you know. Stiff and stodgy schoolmistresses. They always call you by your first and last names, not just by your last name, and certainly never just by your first name.' Humorously faking a very stiff manner of speech, he continued. '"It would be the greatest offence against decorum there if a teacher were to address a student by her Christian name." Very stuffy. Very formal. Nothing for you.'

'Oh, I could handle it all right!' insisted Unity. 'Just let me go.'

Sixteen-year-old Unity Mitford arrived at St Margaret's, just twelve miles or so from London, at the beginning of the school year. The school looked similar to her father's mansion, and the place was hardly less rural than back home, but this was freedom. Here was the promise of freedom from parental supervision. She felt she would finally find companionship with other girls her own age.

Bobo strolled down the corridors and peered into the dormitories. They had beds for sixteen girls in each and curtained cubicles for privacy – the only occasion for privacy. She didn't find it at all fair to discover that the assistant matron supervising every dormitory had a room of her own at the end of the hall, partitioned off.

Unity was quick to show off her drawing skills – mostly nudes, to be shocking.

'You have a real talent for it,' said the girl sitting next to her, watching Unity put pencil to paper. 'I'm Sarah,' she said. 'And you're the new girl.'

'I'm Unity,' she said, curtly shaking hands with the girl before quickly resuming the drawing she seemed so wrapped up in.

After she finished, she looked up at the girl and asked, 'Would you like to see more?'

'Oh yes,' Sarah replied.

Unity opened her rough notebook to reveal naked figures of Adam and Eve. One can guess what they were doing.

The two girls snickered over it, attracting the attention of the teacher, who came over to their desks, taking the notebook out of Bobo's hands with one swift swoop.

Just as swiftly, the teacher flipped through the pages, examining the doodles with a disapproving air. 'You must stop with this obscenity,' she hissed, 'and if you persist, then you shall have to get a new notebook at your own expense.'

This made no impression on disobedient Unity. She stuck her tongue out at the teacher in hideous fashion as soon as her back was facing.

Bobo was simply naughty, thoroughly against the grain, and that was that. She had a potentially ruthless personality, and never let anyone push her around. She had always had the best of everything. Her family was rich and influential. Aristocratic. Bad manners and spoiled behaviour were almost expected from children of her class, and taken as a given. Still, whether a child comes from a well-off background or not, most know when to stop. She didn't.

Bobo and her new best friend at school – her only real friend, in fact – were not in the cliques. They were bullied.

One evening, some of the girls had a special boarding-school trick in store for Unity and Sarah. They waltzed into the dormitory, eight girls strong, and walked over to Unity, who was lying down sideways in bed, reading. Sarah was putting on her make-up.

Unity looked up and gave the clique of girls a mean, suspicious look.

On her nightstand stood a good-luck talisman. 'What the hell is that?' one of the girls sneered. It sounded more like an insult than a question.

Unity very deliberately ignored her, a haughty expression on her face, and continued with her reading.

This infuriated the other girl. 'You must be a witch!' She picked up the talisman and threw it across the room.

'Witch and her sinister little helper!' the other girls chanted. They grabbed Unity and Sarah by both arms and dragged them downstairs, locking them in the bathroom.

'I think we'll just have to leave you in the lavatory overnight!' gasped one of the girls.

Unity could hear their laughter and then their chatter as it became fainter and fainter. She pulled at the door handle as hard as she could, but of course it was no use. 'Bitches!'

'What do we do now?' sighed Sarah in despair.

Unity stared at her for a few moments, and then suddenly, at the top of her voice, let out an ear-splitting scream loud enough to shatter any eardrum.

The assistant matron rushed down and, before Bobo knew it, the janitor had rescued her and her friend from a cold and uncomfortable night with the toilets.

Around midnight, while all the other girls were asleep, Bobo snuck out of bed and shook Sarah, leading her out into the corridor.

'Revenge…' said Unity.

Sarah nodded, half-comprehendingly.

'Come on…'

They slithered into a classroom, Sarah following behind like a puppy ready to take orders from her master. They stole the notebooks of the eight girls who had bullied them earlier, slipping them out of their desks, and ran outdoors, trying to suppress their giggles.

The moon shone down like a great big lamp; it was a bright and starry night, with a dark blue sky. They could see what they were doing without the need for a flashlight.

They buried the notebooks at the edge of the schoolyard.

'Tomorrow they'll get in trouble for losing them!' said Unity with a look of wry glee.

Unity had an insubordinate and individualistic streak. Once there was a class debate about what each student would like to be as an adult. 'I would like to be a power behind the throne,' said Unity coolly, and she said it with an air so confident, it looked prophetic. Some of the girls snickered.

Later, in a Scripture lesson, they read the passage where he who calls his brother a fool is said to be in danger of hellfire. Bobo raised her hand and gasped, 'But suppose that your brother *is* a fool?' There was a burst of laughter around her.

'Put your hand down, Unity Mitford,' was the only answer she got from her sour-faced teacher.

Unity resented the strict, somber religiosity of the school and established an Atheist Society with Sarah and four other students, calling themselves 'The Sinful Six', and referring to themselves as a secret sisterhood of unapologetic heathens and heretics. She pretended to be very atheistic, not necessarily because she didn't believe in God, but because she knew that the matrons who ran the place had a deathly dread of atheism and atheists.

Unity waited until the Sunday services were over before she confronted the priest just as he was descending from the pulpit. 'How do you know God exists?' Bobo asked, rather snappishly. 'And *how* do you know the Bible holds the truth?'

The priest gave her a slightly dumbfounded gesture. 'Because I believe,' he replied feebly.

'I could believe that you're a blooming elephant, but that wouldn't make it so,' she retorted.

A week later, Unity resolved that she would not go to church. She and an accomplice, Mary, hid while the others went. The two of them then gathered together all the radios in the school and took them down into the schoolyard, turning them on full blast, each one playing a different station.

They screamed and laughed, running and dancing around in circles, giggling hysterically as the half-dozen or so radios howled and blared their deafening noise far and wide.

What amounted to a mild 'smack on the hand' from the janitor was all they got, as the principal and all the teachers were off at church the whole time and didn't know of the transgression.

Unity and Sarah left the school grounds after their ten o'clock evening curfew and headed into town. What did they care about the risk of being caught and punished? That was half the thrill.

'I want to buy some cigarettes,' said Unity, having decided that she wanted to try smoking.

They found a kiosk open late and by midnight were back at the school, sitting on the rooftop, huffing and puffing away. They had real *chutzpah*, to use a Yiddish word. Audacity was Unity's middle name, or at least it would have been if her middle name wasn't already Valkyrie. Sarah acted as her blind and wanton follower.

After completely finishing the carton of cigarettes, they threw slates off the roof to the ground below to leave a mess that would annoy the school administration the next morning.

They laughed hysterically and scurried off to hide in the darkness of the school gardens.

Unity wanted to be expelled, but she was only temporarily suspended for rebelling against the school rules and causing various mischief. Obviously, it was not considered a good public relations move to expel the daughter of a high and mighty aristocrat, especially one who paid such a nice big sum for his Unity to attend the institution.

Of course, the suspension was hushed up by her family, who simply said that she was home on holiday.

While at home, Bobo helped out at a charitable function. People who would later know her only for her obsession with Hitler and support for the Nazis could not imagine that hidden underneath the bad, there was so much potential for goodness.

The Reverend Wilfred Float was vicar of All Saints' church and had known the Mitfords for many years. Unity found him sensible and sympathetic, and didn't hold him in disdain, as she did most other religious figures.

'You've always been so charming, ever since you were a little girl,' said the Reverend.

She chuckled. 'The girls back at school don't seem to think so,' she replied. 'The other children have never played with me much. What should I do about it?'

'You wait,' he said. 'One day you may be somebody... and the day may come when you will be able to lord it over them.'

Bobo's older sister Diana was starting to get into Nazism and gave Bobo a swastika. Unity knew nothing about it but asked many questions, and little by little she also started to fall under the spell of fascism.

Unity came back on a visit to St Margaret's, displaying the swastika in her lapel, very pleased with the effect that her new adoration of Hitler had on everyone.

One of them hissed, 'Take it off!'

'Yeah, along with the SMB badge, which you have no right to be wearing anymore, anyway...' added another.

'Oh, you get so full of your own importance!' spat Unity, strutting off.

By that stage, it was unbearable. She wanted out. But she wanted to go out with a bang. A chunky rock broke through the headmistress' bedroom window. The paper taped to it was scrawled with the words, 'From Unity, With Love.' Immediately, this near-debutante found herself sacked from school in her seventeenth year.

Unity didn't much mind not finishing middle school; after all, she reasoned to herself, she would marry some rich man of her own class someday and never have to work anyway. Working for a living. Ugh. So middle-class.

Bobo 'came out' when she was eighteen. Over 200 guests were invited. They danced in an exquisite white ballroom and a first-rate dinner was served on refectory dining tables in several elaborately furnished dining rooms adjoining the main hall, their austere white walls strewn with grand paintings. The note of ornate austerity continued throughout the place. The old walls and arched ceilings had been built in 1760. Good use was also made of the 'old-world' garden by those who wanted to take their partner outside into the balmy summer evening air. It was dark and romantic.

In attendance were maids wearing the charming green and white floral dresses that the hostess, Lady Redesdale, had chosen in place of the usual staid uniforms. Almost anyone who was anyone in society seemed to be there, all decked out and beautifully dressed. This coming-out party appeared very glamorous.

Unity was wearing a gorgeous and slightly risqué frock dress, with grey lace and ruffles. She was very proud of it. She was holding a leather bag in one hand, whose contents she was planning to reveal.

'My, don't we look strange today?' said her mother.

'Yes, don't you,' said Unity coolly, brushing past her.

She joined her sister Jessica, who was talking to a nice and handsome young man named Albert, a tall, blonde and well-built stud whose parents were old family acquaintances.

'Hi Al,' she said sweetly.

'Well hello Unity,' he replied, clearly happy to see her.

Unity knew Albert fairly well. She had had a bit of a crush on him for years.

'Bobo, what's in the bag?' asked Jessica, grimacing.

Unity laughed. 'You know…'

It was her pet grass snake, Enid.

'No, Bobo, you can't…'

'Yes, I will.' Nothing gave Unity a higher thrill than letting the snake loose in a room packed with people and watching everyone act aghast while she just stood there laughing hysterically in the midst of the panic. It gave her the biggest high, like a drug stimulant.

'You mustn't, it's your coming-out... Mother would kill you!'

'Oh don't worry, you. I won't set him loose this time... I just wanted to show him off.'

Suddenly the tiny head and sniffing little nose of her pet rat, Ratular, appeared out of her sleeve.

Albert smiled. 'Can I stroke it?'

'Yes, and you can hold him!' said Unity.

But that was a little more than Albert had in mind. 'Oh that's alright, I just want to touch his fur, if he doesn't bite.'

'She likes to put him in my bath as a joke,' said Jessica, accusingly.

Feeling no tinge of remorse, Unity added to Jessica's remark: 'Usually I just like to wear him on my body, or put him on somebody's shoulder from behind when they don't expect it.'

'Shock exhibitionism. I like that,' said Albert, taking a sip of his champagne while exchanging a prolonged smile with Unity.

This pleased Unity very much, giving her a sweet burning sensation inside her body.

'You have such an innocent face, with china-blue angel eyes, but I have a feeling you were born with the devil in you,' he continued.

She smiled wide, unable to think of a clever response but clearly very amused by his assessment of her.

That night, Unity was noticed a lot. She was so beautiful. She was quieter than her other sisters, and although sometimes quite self-confident and assertive, she was also very shy and aloof. She would not talk to many people, only to herself. Al was the rare exception on that occasion.

'Are you having a good time?' he asked.

'Oh, I prefer fancy-dress parties. They're more fun,' she replied. 'I like to wear strange, gaudy things, and I bring the pet rat too.'

'There was a fancy-dress ball in the Albert Hall recently. The Victoria Palace music hall too. Were you there?' he asked. 'I didn't see you. But you will have many admirers.'

She was grateful for the compliment and felt like kissing him, but instead just said, 'I just like to really stand out at parties. I wear flashy rings, a tiara, capes and velvets from a theatrical costumier – to the annoyance of some of the primmer mothers and others at the dance.'

Al chuckled. 'I can just picture it in my mind.'

'Oh God, he's watching me,' said Unity, referring to a boy named Robin who admired her and whom she didn't like in the least.

'Well, is it any wonder? Half the men in the room have been gawking at you all night. You look like Cinderella.'

Bobo mocked Robin in front of Al. 'Look, he has Chinese eyes. You can see Robin's got Chinese blood. *My* family is pure-bred Aryan.'

'What about me?' asked Al.

'You've got filthy blood, too,' she said with a straight face; then burst out laughing. 'Only joking!'

'Let's dance,' suggested Al.

They waltzed around the room with grace and ease, but Bobo tripped on purpose at one point, so that she could fall into his embrace.

Al laughed and lifted her up with his broad, muscular arms, giving her a chance to grab him tightly. It was heaven to her.

'You did that on purpose?' Jessica gasped in disbelief, rolling her eyes.

'For the sake of being caught and picked up,' Unity explained with a broad smile. 'I adore Al with true devotion.'

Unity and Jessica's favourite little place seemed to be the Harrods pet shop. They enjoyed going there often. It was where Bobo had bought her grass-snake Enid. Everywhere Unity went, Enid went too. Whenever Unity tossed Enid far out into the river, the snake would slither back to shore and her mistress, showing the loyalty of a faithful pet.

Going to deb dances with Enid around her neck became common. She also added Sally the salamander to her menagerie. Her little pet rat Ratular was purchased at Harrods as well. And so was her big black Rottweiler, Rebel. But she didn't like cats. Bobo much preferred having a rat to a cat because she viewed cats as boring, common pets.

All in all, Unity liked animals better than people.

Eighteen years old and almost six feet tall, she was becoming more mature and even sophisticated in some ways – and above all else, a free spirit. Individualism and a lack of inhibition were her hallmark. And to hell with what *people* thought.

Unity was at the swimming pool with her sisters and their friends, talking babies and motherhood, when she blurted out, 'I want to have a lot of sons as cannon-fodder.'

Outraged, Jessica replied, 'I bet you'll only have one and you'll die in childbirth.'

That retort really shut Unity up. She just began to sulk and pout, then after a long contemplative pause, she muttered, 'I don't think I will. I've got very wide hips.'

But it was Jessica who had the last word: 'That doesn't count. The outside measurements don't count.'

Unity just sat there in the pool, frowning and looking miserable. She could not help but be noticed. She heard the others talking about her. She hated to be talked about.

'Your sister's no fun,' said one of the girls. 'Seems pretty queer, silent, melancholy. I wonder if she can laugh or smile.'

'You've never seen Bobo giggle and giggle,' said Jessica, coming to her sister's defence. 'She's funny and has an adorable smile. Really, if anyone loves a good laugh, it's her. But in photographs she looks severe because Diana says smiling wrinkles the skin, so she always puts on her straight photography face and prefers to be photographed facing away from the camera.'

Unity was glad Jessica had said all this. She felt she had a lot of humour that simply didn't come out in the accounts of her.

The girls then started chatting about films and film stars. Unity was very keen on the movies and many thoughts and opinions crossed her mind as she listened to the conversation, but she didn't say anything.

Suddenly, she saw Al approaching. The same Al from her grand coming-out bash.

'Hello, Cinderella,' he said. 'Will I see you at the dance tonight?'

'Of course. I never miss a fancy-dress party. They're my favourite.'

'What will you come as?'

'A shepherdess. And you?'

'Let it be a surprise.' He sighed and smiled.

They started gazing dreamily into each other's eyes, which made Al start to blush. Unity's own shyness made her avert her eyes.

Wanting to keep the conversation going, Al asked her, 'What do you do in your free time?'

'Oh, I detest that old question about hobbies and interests,' she sneered. 'All right, I'll tell you. Since forever, I've liked to sing.'

'What songs?'

'Dirty songs. But also hymns; yes, the Alexander hymns, mission hymns, and so on. This in spite of my atheism,' she confessed. 'I also adore children and look forward to marrying. I have no little nieces, so I like to dress my little nephew up as a girl. I tell him, "When I get married, you're going to be my bridesmaid."'

'Ah, so your primary goal in life is marriage?' he asked.

'Oh, not at all!' she exclaimed, as if slightly offended. 'I aim higher than that. People will not soon forget the name Unity Valkyrie.'

'Valkyrie? What's that?'

'A girl back at school once made fun of my middle name, so I called her a rude ignorant bitch. And that's not all I did.'

'Well, I'm not making fun, and I hope I'm not ignorant. I'm certainly not rude.'

'No, of course not. If you want to know, Valkyrie is a Scandinavian maiden. I like to hope I look the part.'

'What did you do to that girl who made fun of your middle name?'

'I splashed my red punch on the girl's white satin gown.'

'Right-oh,' said Al with a chuckle, nodding.

Again, there was a pause as they dove deeply into each other's eyes for the second time.

'You know, you really are brilliant, the way you caught me from falling that time on the dance floor,' said Unity with a sweet and soft expression that didn't always come easily or naturally. 'It reminds me of the time I went skating. I'm not a very good ice skater either. Tall and awkward. Clumsy. Last winter I fell flat on my face in the skating rink. They asked me why I hadn't put my hands out to soften the blow.'

'What was your answer?'

'I was waiting to see if God would prompt me.'

They both laughed aloud. A resounding guffaw. Unity's sisters and their friends in the pool stopped mid-conversation and turned to gawk at them in silence. Unity could see the jealousy and resentment in their eyes. She wasn't popular like them, but *she* had ultra-desirable Al wrapped around her finger. Not they.

Time passed and Jessica became Communist, while Unity became ever more interested in Nazism. And as she drew away from Jessica, she became closer and closer to her older sister Diana, who continued to guide her towards Mosley and Hitler. Within the next two years, Unity was a fervent fascist and a Nazi supporter.

Unity took some chalk and drew a line in the wood across the middle of the bedroom floor, to symbolise their ideological and personal divide. On her side of the room, Jessica displayed hammers and sickles and large portrait of Stalin and the Soviet flag, while Unity put up her smaller but numerous photographs of Hitler and swastikas in her own half of the room.

Unity's ability to shock satisfied an innate and primordial urge. The rebel in her screamed for release once again. She wanted to be different, unique. To make her mark somehow. To outdo everybody in something. This was the way she felt she could do it, and have a lot of fun at it.

'Jess, you don't know Hitler. I'm sure you'd like him,' said Unity.

'Oh no I wouldn't, and I don't want to know him.'

'I do. And so will you. You just wait and see, Jess. You'll be fighting the Russians.'

Jessica's jaw just about dropped to the floor. Was she joking?

Unity laughed when she saw her sister's expression. Then, hugging her like in the old days when they had been close, she sighed in her ear: 'There, there now, you silly. Don't hate Hitler so much.'

'It's *he* who hates, not me. If you hate the Jews or any other human race, you hate yourself. We're all human.'

'Not them. They're rats,' snarled Unity.

'No, Bobo, no,' said Jessica. 'Besides, you hate them and call them rats but you love *your* rat. That's hypocrisy!'

'No, that's different!' insisted Unity.

'Listen, if you're going to judge the Jews, you need to judge them individually, not broad-brush the whole race and say you hate *all* Jews. That's bloody narrow-minded and wrong. Even *if* some or even many Jews were bad people, for argument's sake, then you still cannot say that of all of them. Therefore, your prejudice is a great injustice to those Jews who happen to be fine, good people. What is more – and this is the strongest point – no one can decide which race they will be born into. It's a matter of blind biological chance. So you cannot blame someone for being born a Jew. They can't help it! In the same way, you cannot pat yourself on the back for being born an Aryan. It was just sheer luck, beyond your control. You could just as easily have been born a savage in Africa. What if a Jew were to come up to you and say that he wishes he had been born an Aryan and beg you to forgive him for being born a Jew? How could you have anything against this man? And would this Jew be right to feel inferior to you? This whole business about a super-race is so much of an absurdity at any rate. There are differences in race and culture, but none is superior to any other by any objective standard... I wonder, if you were put in a kindergarten with scores of beautiful Jewish five-year-olds and then given a gun and told to wipe out that much Jewry, would you do it?'

'Theoretically speaking, yes I would,' was her chilly reply. 'You have to understand, it's us or the Jews. That's the stark choice we're ultimately faced with.'

Lord Redesdale didn't like his daughters' support of Nazism and communism, but as a passive and mild-mannered individual, he left it alone. He certainly didn't dare challenge Unity, fond father that he was. His wife, their mother, was usually the disciplinarian, but she would defend them, saying, 'This is nothing more than pantomime; they're just play-acting as children do, and you need to understand that it's only play.'

But of course there are childhood games that can have grave consequences in adult life.

The family was now living in Swinbrook village, Oxfordshire, where Lord Redesdale had bought a new and more spacious mansion. The locale was even more secluded than their previous home, and Unity was soon feeling isolated and bored.

As hard as life had been for Unity among her schoolmates, it was not much easier in her big family. Most of her sisters were older, and better than her in just about every way. Just out of her teens, Unity began to notice this more and more. Her sister Nancy had written several popular novels. Jessica was starting to make a name for herself as a gifted newspaper journalist. Diana was well known and admired for her beauty and as a prominent and entertaining socialite in high-society circles. But what had she, Unity, done? Bobo was struggling to find her place in the scheme of things.

She felt depressed about it and took Rebel for a walk along the River Windrush. It was getting dark out and the dark purple sky with its darkening air only fed the sadness. Unity strolled down the path beside the water and wondered if she shouldn't just drown herself. But no, she reasoned, her dog would try to save her. The thought put a half-smile on her face and cheered her up momentarily. At least somebody cared about her, even if it wasn't a human being. Then she realised how devastating her suicide would be to her loving and beloved father, and the thought fled her mind.

But her melancholy remained, because she thought to herself, *I'm just not good enough. Too many talented and accomplished siblings. How can I stand out among them in any way? How can I show that I matter?* It was then and there that Unity decided she was going to do the one thing she had a true talent for: she would be a nonconformist, a rebel, the one who dares to say and do what others won't. It was true, she thought, that people liked her knack for drawing and that she could dance and ride a horse fairly well, but these were not exceptional abilities in her case. In order to compete with the others, she needed to do something *more*, much more. She needed to *become* someone. And if she couldn't achieve it through her own abilities, then there had to be other ways to gain fame or notoriety for herself.

Coming back from her stroll, she sat down in front of her beauty mirror and studied every feature of her face long and hard. She thought about how her physical looks were the exact ideal of female beauty for the Nazis. Her large, gorgeous, blue eyes; her tall, buxom frame; her straight and shiny blonde hair, sometimes in a neat bun or done in braids, but more often cascading loose over her shoulders – all made her look like a Viking goddess. Finally, she felt truly accepted. She saw that she would be welcomed and liked by these people and their nationalist cause.

Nobody should tease me about my devotion to fascism, Unity thought – *or else!* She was becoming utterly brainwashed, completely in their camp.

Bobo never knew any Jews, had next to no experience of Jews. As far as she knew she had never even met a Jew, yet she was sure as sure can be that she hated the Jews. Every Jew. She filled her mind with anti-Semitic propaganda. Her hatred grew and became as vehement as it was irrational. A classic case of hatred born of ignorance. Her first-hand experience of Jews amounted to nothing more than one or two Jewish men seen at society parties, and at a ball held by Lady Rothschild. But she didn't really *know* any Jews. They were almost as alien to her as UFOs. They were very easy for her to marginalise and despise.

The next morning, when the postmistress rang the doorbell to deliver a package, the maid had the day off so Unity answered the door and gave the startled postmistress the Nazi salute: 'Heil Hitler!' she said, with her hand raised. This was her new standard greeting to anyone and everyone – family, friends, the astonished postmistress in Swinbrook, whoever. Soon she would come to be teased and ridiculed as being 'even more Nazi than the Nazis'.

Unity's old friend from school, Sarah, came to visit. They hadn't seen each other since her expulsion.

They hugged madly and blabbed on and on to catch up. Everything went so smoothly at first. But then Unity asked Sarah out of the blue, 'Are you a fascist or a communist?'

'Neither. I'm a democrat, I suppose.'

'Well, that's not as bad as communism, but it's bad enough. Democracy is founded on greed and corruption – the natural breeding ground for the Jews.'

Sarah was disturbed by the remark. She had Jewish friends, and she herself was, in fact, half-Jewish on her mother's side. This Unity did not know. 'I don't know, Jews seem to me no different than anyone else,' mumbled Sarah, somewhat nervously.

Unity sneered aloud and gave her an ugly expression. 'Thank the gods that I have nothing to do with any rotten Jews, for I don't know how I could keep up appearances if I were to find out that someone I know is one. "England for the English, out with the Jews!" That's my motto.' Then she started chanting in a sing-songy way, 'The Yids, the Yids, we've got to get rid of the Yids…'

Sarah tried to protest that this was wrong but Unity became quite upset. 'Oh, shut up! If you are a Jew-lover, I don't see how we can remain friends…'

Back at school, Sarah had fallen in love with Unity's personality, her rare brand of eccentricity and her refreshingly rebellious nature, and she felt a kind of loyalty that she wanted to preserve in spite of their now very real differences. But there was a change in Unity. A sinister change. Why had she adopted this strongly anti-Semitic worldview? Unity had never so much as mentioned the Jews when they were attending St Margaret's together. This was new to Sarah. This was not rebellion in the name of freedom and individuality as before, but rather evil and bigotry. Sarah was speechless and didn't know what to say. She just sat there, mute and alienated. Unity couldn't help but notice.

Remembering their old friendship, Unity felt a tinge of remorse for her last outburst, and added, 'Oh come now, Sarah, you must be a fascist. When the revolution comes and Mosley's blackshirts take power here in England, you want to be on the right side, the winning side, surely?'

Members of the British Union of Fascists (BUF) were popularly known as the blackshirts, and Oswald Mosley was their leader.

Bravely, Sarah stood her ground, even though she looked timid and uncomfortable. After all, she had always been the submissive one in the relationship, and it was very difficult for her to stand up to Unity. 'I suppose we'll simply have to be prepared to fight on opposing sides,' she said.

Unity mused glumly. 'All right then. But I wonder what it will be like if one day I would have to give the order for your execution.'

When Sarah's visit was over, Unity hoped they would never see each other again.

Unity and her family were invited to an immense luncheon party at a luxurious estate in the affluent Hyde Park Gardens. It was hosted by a rich Jewish financier and jeweller and his wife – the Rothensteins. They were an elderly and well-respected couple.

At the dining table, Emily Rothenstein seemed to Unity ancient, ugly, disgusting. There was of course no possible comparison between this decrepit hag and her own youth and prettiness. It was like the difference between black and white. *How horrid it must be to grow old!* thought Unity.

But the worst was yet to come. If the woman's looks were bad enough, what came out of Emily's mouth when she opened her mouth to speak was ten times worse.

'I'm certain that the English are one of the lost tribes of Israel,' said Mrs Rothenstein.

Unity immediately began mocking her in hushed whispers, which was embarrassing for those who had to endure her rudeness. Yet no one had the sense to stop her. Apparently, they seemed to find the old woman's remarks just as ridiculous as Unity's brazen impoliteness.

At one point the old woman seemed to forget what she was talking about in a moment of senile confusion, and then decided on a tangent about 'that horrible little bald Italian man, Mussolini. Why, he's a mad dictator, as you may know.'

Unity rolled her eyes and exhaled aloud in irritation, for the first time hinting strongly at her feelings towards her hostess. But poor Mrs Emily Rothenstein didn't seem to notice, or care.

'But you know,' the old woman added, 'he's not quite as bad as Hitler, since Mussolini at least has Jewish friends and is not an enemy of the Jews.' Almost in the same breath she started talking about her last trip to Italy and her so-called 'extraordinary encounters' while staying at a hotel in Perugia. She said she had been inspired to write a novel.

Unity muttered in a low but audible tone, 'If her novel is like her conversation, I should think it is wearisome.'

Mrs Rothenstein became quite animated. 'Oh, I had such an adventure there. I went out in the evening and found myself in a dark, dark little alleyway. A man going across with a Roman lamp stopped and turned and watched me and I watched him, frozen… Oh, now *that* is what I call an adventure!'

Unity snarled: 'My God! She is so gushing about *nothing*.'

The old woman then lit a cigarette. 'A woman at my age smoking, how perfectly dreadful.' She chuckled.

She smoked like a chimney – or like Churchill – and continued to tell what she called 'most amusing stories'. No one felt that they were, and she appeared to be the only one amused.

But as bad of an impression as Mrs Rothenstein made, Unity made an even more disagreeable one. Her lack of manners was appalling, and was certainly considered far outside the social norm. Her brother Tom was also a fascist, but was embarrassed by his sister's blatantly rude treatment of Mrs Rothenstein. He made this evident.

After the evening was over and everyone was leaving to their cars, Tom abruptly came up to Unity in the street from behind and roughly yanked her by the elbow. She turned to face him, startled. He was not afraid to voice his displeasure: 'You're hideous. Head of bone and heart of stone…'

Sick of home once again, Unity enrolled in the art school of the London County Council in Vincent Square. There she befriended Mary Ormsby-Gore, one of the few people she would treat as an equal. 'Gore', as Unity called her, would take the place of her former friend, Sarah.

Unity and Mary wanted to join the blackshirts. Diana Mitford had become the mistress of the British fascist leader, Oswald Mosley, in the same year that Unity had 'come out' as a debutante. Diana even abandoned her own husband for Mosley. Unity started fantasising about going one better than her sister – by seducing Hitler.

Their mother, the strict Lady Redesdale, flew into a rage over the disgrace and ordered everyone in the family never to see Diana or '*that man* Mosley' ever again. The rebellious Unity disobeyed and that summer secretly met with Mosley at a party thrown by Diana. Mosley was touched by her courageous loyalty and bestowed upon her the party emblem.

Unity and Mary were in Eaton Square, London, on a Saturday afternoon and all of a sudden saw a fascist selling blackshirt uniforms. They jumped at the chance to buy theirs.

'I know the Leader of the party personally, you know,' Unity boasted. The fascist vendor was clearly thrilled to hear it.

With the long black dress and uniform, Mary and Unity were ecstatic with joy. 'Now we can properly march in a fascist parade!' Bobo gasped.

She now had a blackshirt uniform in one hand and a basket of luscious, fresh strawberries in the other. Pam, a friend of Unity's mother, had given her the basket to pass along to Lady Redesdale. This 'extra baggage' now annoyed Unity.

When Unity spotted a jeweller's shop, she and Mary went inside. Placing the strawberry basket on top of the counter, she said to the clerk of the store, 'I want to have this safety chain fitted on my party emblem given to me by the leader from his own coat.'

The clerk smiled. 'That won't be a problem. I'll have it done for you by tomorrow morning.'

This meant everything to Unity; the strawberries meant nothing. Absent-mindedly, she turned around and left the store, forgetting the strawberries.

Her mother criticised her non-stop as soon as she found out about it. 'That's the trouble with you, you never thinking about what you're doing!'

'Oh, be reasonable,' sighed Unity. 'You'll have your bloody strawberries tomorrow!'

But when Unity got up early the next day to retrieve the basket, the shop clerk told her, 'I'm sorry, but I had to eat them or they would have gone rotten.'

Unity became irate at the jeweller, quite furious. 'I would bet that *you* are a rotten Jew! What you did is stealing!' She stormed out of the shop.

The next day, Unity went to the local branch of the BUF at 6 King Edward Street and she enthusiastically proclaimed with conviction, 'I want to be a fascist!' The man at the desk was the branch head, Vincent Keens. He was taken aback and a little speechless. 'Well, I'm in the right place aren't I?' said Unity. 'These are your party headquarters, aren't they?'

Keens sighed. 'Well, yes… But I must confess to you that several undesirable girls have been pestering to join the party simply to flirt and have fun with "the boys" and I fear that you may be one of them.'

'Well my interest is purely political. And I assure you I'm not one of *those* girls at all, sir. In fact, I'm the daughter of Lord Redesdale. And my sister Diana is—'

'Yes, yes, I know,' he interrupted, well aware of Mosley's relationship with Diana, and very pleasantly surprised that Unity was her sister. Unity saw Keens's expression soften considerably and it immediately became clear to her that he would be happy to welcome such a genuinely upper-class and well-connected article as Unity Mitford to the party ranks. So Unity became an official member of the British Union of Fascists.

After leaving the branch offices, Unity was walking down the street when she was approached by a poor old woman who looked Jewish. On her back was a heavy bundle.

'Can you tell me the way to the railway station?' she asked Unity.

Unity, seeing how heavy the bundle was, decided to give the woman wrong directions as a cruel joke.

'Wasn't that wonderful of me?' She laughed to Mary.

Wherever Unity now went, she had on her blackshirts uniform and carried in her pocket a yo-yo, with which she loved to kill time. But the blackshirts emblem was not enough – she had a swastika in her buttonhole, too.

A young girl at the art school pounced on Unity. 'It's shocking that you're wearing that!' she said.

'If you had any sense, you'd be wearing it too,' Bobo coolly retorted. 'When Hitler makes Mosley our Prime Minister, Jews will be made to eat grass. I am in favour of Jews eating grass. Under our regime, women will not need lovers. They will have multiple husbands and great quantities of healthy Aryan children. So you see how much better life will be for *both* of us.'

'A Jew was attacked and beaten up on the street last night by some blackshirt ruffians. You can't be in favour of that, surely,' said the girl.

'Jolly good, serves him right. We should have gone and cheered,' said Bobo with utter nonchalance.

Unity went on vacation to Paris with her sister Jessica and her mother. They met the lesbian wit Dolly Wilde, the niece of the even wittier Oscar Wilde.

Jessica and Unity had a ball trying to flirt with and pretending to seduce Dolly as she sat between them in a taxi. They ran their hands and fingers under her fur coat and up her dress. It was a competition to see which one of them could touch her private parts first. Unity won.

Bobo laughed when she saw how mad with anger it was making her mother to see them acting this way. 'Girls, stop that at once!' said Lady Redesdale.

Unity ignored her mother and tried to drown out her protests by singing aloud her own satirised version of a popular hit song that was continuously played on the radio that year. She changed a few of the words so that the song would be about Dolly:

Goodbye Dolly, I must leave you,
Though it breaks my heart to go.
Goodbye Dolly, I must leave you
For the front to face the foe.
All the soldier boys are marching …

When they got back to their *pension* rooms, Unity pinned a picture of Hitler on the wall and saluted it.

'You look so stupid doing that!' said Jessica.

'You look stupid doing anything,' Unity murmured.

That night, Unity was talking in her sleep and screamed out. She hated to be alone. She wished she could invite handsome SS and SA officers to keep her company in bed. But she knew how shocked her mother and the maid would be. She knew they already thought she was mad enough.

Unity wasn't very fond of the French and insisted that they proceed to Berlin, where she had an expatriate pen-friend named Derek Hill, whom she wanted to meet. Derek was a seventeen-year-old studying stage design. Unity was older than him, but was not above his maturity level.

She telephoned as soon as they were in Berlin and he showed the Mitfords around the city. There were also picnics in the countryside and trips to baroque churches and on the Danube. Derek also took her further afield. They backpacked on trains and buses like university students. After their travelling exertions, they loved to stop at the Café Heck at the end of the day. Unity fell madly in love with the blackforest cakes with whipped cream. She always wanted another piece but sighed, 'No I can't, I'm fat enough already.'

Before long, with Derek's help, Unity knew Berlin like the back of her hand. She served as her mother's guide and suggested they take the tram to pass the statue of Hitler so that they could give it the Nazi salute.

'No!' replied her mother.

Unity felt peeved and insulted by this response, so when she saw her mother wasn't looking, she slipped out of the tram at the next stop and took off, leaving her mother to find her own way back to their *pension*.

Unity read in the newspapers about a woman who had fallen down at Hitler's feet to embrace and kiss his boots. She had lay there on her knees before him with the gravel on her lips, euphoric.

Bobo felt something like the first stirrings of an orgasm reading about that. As a power figure, as a symbol of popularity, as an object of every Aryan woman's sexual desire, Hitler had an incredible appeal. The women screamed and groaned, wept and fainted in ecstasy, for this impotent, middle-aged bachelor.

Ah, Unity. The poor little rich girl whose debutante experiences amounted to more brawls than balls, and she seemed proud of it, too. The big rebel. Her thirst for rebellion was ultimately quenched by Nazism. But it's important to grasp Unity in all of her contradictions. Fanatical and eccentric as she was, she was also fascinating. Her closest friend and confidante, Mary, also wanted to study German in Germany. They wanted to room and board together.

Finding out that Hitler spent most of his time in Munich, Unity and Mary moved to Munich and began taking German lessons every other day from a private tutor named Fräulein Baum, reputed to be an excellent German teacher for foreigners. If she was going to become 'Hitler's girl', Bobo knew she first had to learn to speak his language.

Baum was wheelchair-bound and her pupils never saw her except behind the teaching desk. Through sheer determination and brains she had become a sought-after success.

Unity arrived for her first lesson and took a seat beside her new teacher. Her first impression of the woman was not good. Unity wasn't impressed by her physical looks. Although nicely dressed, Baum had brownish skin, jet-black hair and Slavic features. *She looks like a Romanian gypsy*, thought Unity. Bobo also felt uncomfortable about a nasty-looking black cat with big yellow eyes crouched on a chair beside her. It watched her with suspicion and a wicked, hypnotic glare.

Soon, Bobo and Baum were discussing the latest books and films and getting along fine.

'I have a strong feeling my German will improve quickly and dramatically under your tutelage,' said Unity after their first lesson finished.

Unity attended the most influential Nuremberg Party Rally, the one in 1933, and saw Hitler on the podium for the first time. His powerful dynamism in front of the microphone was the most electrifying experience imaginable.

The atmosphere was electric. The crowd went crazy, absolutely wild with adulation for the Führer. The extreme degree of excitement and electricity in the air was not possible to adequately put into words. Unity was already in love with Hitler, but this was love transformed into idol-worship.

Unity had stars in her eyes and was all a-twitter. She turned to Mary and moaned, 'Oh God, Gore, isn't the Führer simply divine today?'

She rushed home immediately when it was over and wrote her father a very rambling and highly enthusiastic letter. 'To me, Hitler is the greatest man in all of world history,' she gushed.

That night, Unity had a dream.

She comes down for breakfast. Her father is waiting at the foot of the great staircase. He gives her his arm and with much ceremony leads her to the dining room, where fragrant roses stand surrounding her plate. She's smothered by hugs and showered with praise by all those present. Her soul is at peace and full to the brim with sweet contentment.

'I feel like I've been turned into a beautiful queen of hearts by some miraculous magic!' she ejaculates, clasping her hands together, as if in prayerful thanks.

Her father replies, 'Well if you wish it, you may be a princess at least. Prince Troubinsky is asking to marry you.'

'Vladimir? That old Vladimir Troubinsky?' The blossoming contentment in her heart wilts and dies in a flashing instant.

'Yes. And so is Oswald Mosley,' says her sister Diana with a jealous, bitter half-grin.

'Both the Russian Prince Troubinsky and the English baronet, Sir Mosley? Aristocracy both here and abroad are after me? Can I be so universally desirable? How incredible!' Then with a searching glance at her father, she continues jokingly, 'Is that all? No one else wants me?'

Her father lifts his eyes, which suddenly become animated. 'Yes,' he says, 'there is another. The Führer, Adolf Hitler, wants you as his beloved wife!'

Her mother suddenly breaks in with a snide laugh: 'Ha! Clearly not one of them is in his right mind!'

The Führer! The Führer! The Führer! It clangs like a bell in her ears. *I shall be Hitler's wife! The most fortunate, most envied, most beloved girl in all creation, with the promise of endless happiness as far as the eye can see!* All the women of the world – poor unlucky girls who had never won the love of the Führer – would want nothing more than to be her, but would not be able to be. Her radiance would overshadow them all. By his side she would sit tall and proud, wallowing in a life of happy serenity, elated in his love, snug under the safe, protective blanket of his power.

'I'm hoping and guessing that you won't choose *that man* Mosley.' Her father frowns, and then smiles.

'Of course not, papa. Oh papa dear, if you want your precious little Bobo to live a life of true happiness, you have to let her marry the Führer!'

'Never!' her father shouts, slamming his fist down. It's so out of character for him to deny her anything, or to show such emotion, that Bobo is stunned by his reaction.

She turns pale. 'Oh, you're horrid to me, papa! Horrid! If you don't let me marry Hitler, I shall kill myself!'

Suddenly, the dream shifts to a wedding scene and the reception afterwards.

'Oh, don't worry yourself with what the tiresome old rotter thinks,' says Hitler to his new English bride, looking much annoyed by her gloomy mood. But she loves her father and his opinions and feelings are important to her. She yearns for his approval.

Diana begs the Führer to be sweet and tender with Unity, and to be understanding. 'Look after her and love her. Don't let her perish of a broken heart,' says Diana. 'She's still such a child in some ways…'

'Yes, yes, yes, of course,' says the Führer, 'but don't think I'm not ready for it. I'll pull her by the ears if she's naughty.'

'And what if I'm a well-behaved little angel?' says Unity.

'In that case you'll get candies and kisses!' And he laughs.

'Promise me, Adolf, that you will always love me and no one else.'

'Only you and no other, ever,' he replies, kissing Unity's hand, on which the new wedding ring shines.

Unity is really enjoying the dream, but abruptly the honeymoon is over, and the nightmare of married life begins.

'Wolfie, you never say anything about my looks. I try to look so pretty for you. Didn't you even notice my new hairstyle?'

'Oh shut up about your hair,' says Hitler. 'You're being tiresome. Don't be such a bore.' And he gives her a quick peck on the cheek, which one wouldn't call much of a kiss.

Bobo kneels down by the bedside to say her prayers.

He grabs her arm.

'What are you doing now?'

'I never forget my evening prayers.'

'I don't want you wasting your time on prayers,' he says. 'I should be your object of worship, not some God. Besides, I thought you told me you were an atheist.'

'It is to *you* I pray,' she says.

Hitler bursts out laughing and gives her a benevolent and forgiving stare.

She smiles back at him, feeling that she has conquered his love again. But her heart sinks into her stomach as he opens his mouth with the same, undying refrain: 'Oh Lord, you really are very tiresome.' He groans and then gives out a whopping yawn. 'You bore me to extinction.'

Unity starts weeping convulsively and then faints on the spot.

Ironically, Hitler becomes alarmed. He summons everyone to her rescue. He calls the finest doctor he knows. Bending over the couch in front of her, on his knees, with his face buried in her lifeless hand, Hitler sobs like an old woman, just like the time his dearly beloved mother died when he was a small child. 'Save her! She is dead! I have killed her!'

Unity's hand moves slowly and her fingers softly caress his hair. 'I'm not dead, my darling,' she says in a gentle voice.

He throws himself upon her and kisses her. 'I love you,' Hitler exclaims like a madman, 'I love you just as you are!'

Unity told Mary her amazing dream at breakfast the next morning. 'It was a prophecy. The Führer is destined to be mine.'

'A prophetic dream? Maybe. But if you want the Führer, you have to win his heart in real life, not just wait for this dream, which otherwise may or may not come true,' said Mary. 'In other words, you must meet him.'

'That's easier said than done,' sighed Unity.

'I'm sure it can be done. And then you simply have to make him fall in love with you.'

'Oh, and *that* will be easy enough too, won't it?' said Unity sarcastically.

'Well there are various possible ways of getting him after you've met,' said Mary. 'What if you try being very affectionate?'

'I'm sure that would bore him to tears.'

'What about being cool and aloof, acting like he means nothing to you?'

'He probably wouldn't take any heed of it,' said Unity.

'What if you act all obsessed and hysterical?'

'Oh Gore, I'm sure that would get me *very* far!'

'Seriously, there are some men who cannot stand healthy, normal women. They like it when a woman behaves as though she cannot live without him. It gives a rise to their ego. Men like Hitler have a large ego. And if that fails, you can try fainting dramatically. It's an age-old method that has always done the trick for us ladies.'

'Oh God, Gore, you're being ridiculous,' said Unity with a pout.

'All right then, bye-bye,' said Mary abruptly, reaching for her hat.

Unity saw that her friend had taken offence. 'No, no! Don't go! Come on, don't abandon me in this before it's resolved!' Unity implored. 'Please, can't you suggest another idea, some different solution?'

'You can try being his sunshine.'

Unity rolled her eyes, losing patience. 'What do you mean by "his sunshine"? That's the kind of term one reads in sappy, sentimental romance novels.'

Mary didn't take offence this time, but explained that if she wanted to be the sunshine of his life she would need to act happy and sparkle in every moment that she was in his presence. 'Wear pretty, light colours. Tie your hair with a pretty ribbon. When you hear the front door open and he comes in, run to greet him. Squeeze your body into his and surprise his lips with a passionate kiss. When he goes out, throw him a flower from your balcony. When he seems bored or depressed, string a guitar and sing for him.'

'That's hopeless. I can't play guitar.'

'Who cares? The singing is the thing that really matters. And you *can* sing. The atmosphere around him should be bright with your sunshine. And you must always keep him basking in this dazzling ray of sunshine.'

'I can imagine doing all you say, and the Führer becoming all bewildered and asking me what's got into me and what in the world am I wearing! I start singing for him and he leaves, and from my bedroom window I toss a tulip to him, which falls on the pavement before him, but he pretends not to notice – and then he's gone who-knows-where for days on end.' Unity smirked cynically.

'Well, in any case, it's useless talking about all this until you've actually met and seduced him!' said Mary with a smile.

'Is such a thing even possible, I wonder?' Unity mused aloud, aimlessly twirling a string of her hair with her finger, her face fixed in a blank expression of deep contemplation, and her thoughts tinged with a feeling of hopelessness.

ove: **1.** Asthall Manor, Unity's
dhood home.

ht: **2.** Unity as a little girl.

ow: **3.** An early family
tograph, with Unity at the bottom

Top: 4. Unity wearing her swastika brooch.

Bottom: 5. Unity and her sisters.

Top: **6.** Unity with her best friend, Mary.

Middle: **7.** Unity with her sisters Diana and Jessica.

Bottom and next page: **8 & 9.** Unity in her beloved Blackshirts uniform.

Above left: 10. Unity and Diana giving the Nazi salute.

Above right: 11. Jessica, Unity's anti-fascist communist sister.

Below: 12. Unity as the Hitler fanatic and groupie, her bedroom wall strewn with pictures of the Führer.

Above left: **13.** A later family photograph with Unity seated front centre, looking away from the camera.

Above right: **14.** Unity with her parents in front of the Osteria Bavaria, Hitler's favourite restaurant, where she first met and became friends with him.

Left: **15.** Unity looking like the Nazi (Nordic) ideal of female beauty.

16. Unity shared Hitler's love of dogs.

Above: **17.** Unity with Streicher, the infamous anti-Semitic newspaper publisher, with whom she had a close relationship.

Right: **18.** The painting of Hitler that he gave Unity as a gift.

19. Hitler seated Unity right beside Eva Braun, knowing of the jealous rivalry between them over him. Unity reacted by trading seats with someone else and sat behind in the next row.

Above left: **20.** Unity listening respectfully to Hitler's table talk.

Above right: **21.** This was one of Unity's favourite photographs.

Left: **22.** Unity was teased and criticised by Hitler and his circle for wearing lipstick and make-up, which was viewed as unbecoming on an Aryan girl.

Below: **23.** Unity and her sister Diana with a group of Nazi soldiers.

24. Unity with her mother at a party held by the Anglo-German League.

Middle and bottom:
25 & 26. Unity upon her return to England after the unsuccessful suicide attempt of shooting herself in the head.

INANITY FARE

You can't criticise Unity
With impunity.
If you try to belittle 'er
You have to answer to Hitler

Left: 27. Unity became the target of parody, criticism, and downright attack in the British press for her Nazi sympathies and friendship with the Führer.

Above right: 28. The small island of Inchkenneth, which was Unity's home and refuge in her last years.

Below: 29. Unity's bedroom was on the top floor of this mansion.

Top and middle: **30 & 31.** The ruins of the ancient chapel on Inchkenneth where Unity used to go to pray and worship.

Bottom: **32.** Unity's grave.

WITH HITLER
AND THE NAZIS

Unity was having her hair cut and styled at her hairdresser's in Bogenhausen, spilling her guts out about her fondness for the Führer.

The hairdresser astonished her when he said, 'If you want to meet him you can, quite easily. He's in the restaurant Osteria every day.'

'Where?' she gulped.

'The Osteria Bavaria. It's his favourite restaurant here in Munich. You can sit there and wait for him to show up.'

The Osteria Bavaria was a nice, trendy, cozy little place. It had a long table that seated eight or more people and the restaurant owner would get telephone calls letting him know when Hitler was coming so that the table would be vacant for him. The back of the restaurant opened into a courtyard outside, which had another big table under a pergola, and Hitler liked to sit out there when pleasant weather prevailed.

Unity and Mary entered the Osteria Bavaria for lunch. They checked out the menu.

'The food is cheap and good,' said Unity, 'I'll go here from now on.' It was a typical German lunch of sausages with rye bread.

Herr Deutelmoser, the restaurant owner, was a sweet old bachelor. He must have taken a liking to Unity. He sent some fresh fruit to her table as dessert, free of charge.

The gesture pleased Unity very much. 'I think I shall just have to love him,' she said.

Unity became fast friends with the two waitresses who worked there, Fräulein Rosa and Fräulein Ella. Unity wouldn't stop asking them about Hitler.

'After my engagement,' said Ella, 'Hitler gave me a wedding reception. "You've served me for so long," he said, "now I'll serve you." It was so touching!'

Unity decided to sit there all day if necessary, until Hitler came. She sat there and read a book to pass the time.

Mary wanted to go, but Unity wouldn't hear of it. 'I don't want to make a fool of myself by being here alone. So stay and keep me company. Have some more tea or a cup of coffee.'

Unity had chosen a table situated in such a way that whoever came into the restaurant would have to pass hers. She wanted to be sure not to miss his arrival, and to get as close as possible to him without bringing obvious attention to it.

Less than an hour later, like clockwork, Unity glanced over to the front part of the restaurant through the corner of her eye and quickly shut her book and put it down as the unmistakable frame of Hitler came into her view. Hitler and his entourage strolled past her without anyone seeming to even notice her existence, and seated themselves at Hitler's table. Unity couldn't help but sense this, and she didn't like it.

When she spoke with Mary now, she started talking with a louder voice and finally she even dropped her book with a noisy thump, making it look like an accident.

This had little effect. A bolder move was in order. Bobo began 'making eyes' at the Führer. Eventually, she saw that he couldn't help but take notice of her. It worked.

Hitler instructed his henchman, Minister of Propaganda Joseph Goebbels, to go over to her and find out who she was. This was the sort of thing that Unity had been waiting and hoping for all along.

'You can go now,' Bobo muttered to Mary, who hurried off.

Unity said to Goebbels, 'I'm just an English... the daughter of an English lord actually... I'd really like to meet him.'

Goebbels went back to Hitler's table and conveyed her message, and Hitler chuckled and smiled. 'Well, invite her to our table then.'

With great politeness and cavalier manners, Hitler kissed her hand and ushered her to a chair right beside him. He first asked her some basic questions: 'Who are you? What are you doing here?'

Unity was a little nervous at first, stuttering in her imperfect German: 'I'm an English student... and I s-so adore you... and I am such a strong supporter of what you've been doing here in Germany.'

Hitler appeared to be immediately intrigued and bedazzled by her.

After such a long time of dreaming about meeting Hitler, Unity was finally in the presence of her idol, a mere inch away from him. Not only that, but she was literally the centre of his attention! They spoke for over an hour, and Hitler paid for Unity's meal.

She then ran back to her flat, where Mary was waiting for her, and they embraced enthusiastically as soon as she came in through the door, thrilled that their plan had come off so well. They were like giddy schoolgirls after a first date. Unity raved about everything that happened to the minutest detail. Even the most frivolous and mundane trivia to do with Hitler was of immense importance to her.

Bobo then sat down at her writing desk and wrote her father and Diana long 800-word letters describing what had happened. She could hardly contain her excitement, as her handwriting indicated. 'This has been the most wonderful and beautiful day of my life,' she wrote. 'I am so happy that I wouldn't mind a bit dying. I suppose I am the luckiest girl in the world.' Again, as she had done similarly once before, she wrote, 'For me he is the greatest man of all time.'

The next day was cold and overcast, pouring buckets, but Unity wouldn't have missed her Osteria Bavaria lunch for the world. Hitler appeared in a big raincoat, with his German Shepherd on a leash in one hand and a whip in the other.

Bobo was instantly excited, and blurted out to Mary, 'He looks so manly and strong. And don't you think his piercing bright blue eyes are marvellous?'

As soon as he saw her, Hitler invited them to his table.

From the beginning, Unity was making a strong, positive impression on the Führer. Bobo was a niece of *the* Winston Churchill and told him, 'I was conceived at a Canadian goldmine owned by my father, ironically called Swastika Mine. Would you believe that? But it's true.'

And it was true. A year before her birth, in 1913, her parents had been to Canada digging for gold at a small town in Ontario called Swastika.

'Another thing I find most intriguing is that your middle name is Valkyrie... That's the name of the war maidens in Wagner's opera. I happen to have a long-time obsession with Wagner's music,' Hitler confessed.

'It may also astonish you to know that my grandfather was a close friend of Wagner. He even translated English books on racial theory into German.'

'Oh really. What was his name?'

'Houston Stewart Chamberlain.'

'My God, that's unbelievable!' Hitler exclaimed. 'That man's book had a tremendous impact on me and even inspired me to write *Mein Kampf*!'

Unity could see that all these links between her and Swastika, Wagner, Aryan racist ideology and so on were making a truly powerful impression on Hitler. It made her feel fantastic inside.

But in spite of the wonderful way Hitler was treating her, she also sensed from his inner circle around them that she was being looked on with quiet suspicion. Goering, Himmler and Hess didn't even try to make conversation with her. Was it jealousy?

Or did they think she might be a spy? At one point, Unity was stung to hear Frau Himmler whisper about her, 'She's just a good-for-nothing devotee.'

But Hitler liked her a lot, and, after all, that was all that mattered. Her company and conversation really contrasted refreshingly with that of his associates.

She talked better than anyone about all the things that he liked to talk about when he was in relaxation mode. She told him about her dog, he told her about his; she thought of herself as musical and arty, so did Hitler; he drooled over Wagner operas and Renoir nudes, so did Unity; they both were in love with the cinema and could talk non-stop about actors and actresses.

Interestingly, Unity's anti-Semitism was even more pronounced than that of most Nazis. 'I read in *Der Stürmer* that you're friends with that Jew Stephanie Hohenlohe,' Unity complained. 'Here you are, anti-Jewish, yet you have a Jew around you the whole time, this Princess Hohenlohe. That kind of inconsistency could look hypocritical and do harm to your political reputation.'

It was true and there was absolutely nothing he could say. Hitler didn't reply; he looked defeated, wounded, dumbstruck, unable to respond. This was almost unheard-of – somebody actually not afraid to speak their mind with the Führer, and, moreover, the great Führer unable to react.

Unity began to break a sweat and fear that she had gone too far, fear that maybe he wouldn't like her anymore.

But Hitler by now held her in such high esteem that, amazingly, all he could eventually utter was, 'Based on all that you say, and based on all that you've revealed to me about yourself, I'm convinced that fate has brought you to me. It didn't happen just by chance.' He nodded slowly.

At their subsequent meetings, Unity was eager to broach the subject of women, romantic/erotic intimacy, and marriage.

She was amused and couldn't erase her smile when Hitler tried to explain to her how there was practically no difference between English and German women except for language and skin. 'If English girls have such pale skin as they say, it is the fault of the English rain.' Unity had white skin, but with a slight healthy shade of pink.

Unity tried to discuss marriage with Hitler, but he cut her short, saying, 'You know, my staff put a few spies on you to track you, and this morning I receive on my desk a report about you which tells me that you're no security risk... but perhaps a moral one, yes.'

'What do you mean, my Führer?' said Unity.

'To be blunt, my informers tell me you're in the habit of picking up Nazi soldiers and taking them back to your rooms. Forgive me, but my political reputation, as you call it, does not allow me to get wedded to a woman who has bedded half my army. Besides, I should tell you from the outset, I'm completely celibate. I have to be, so that I remain desirable to all German women. If I ever made the mistake of marrying one, all the rest of them would stop wanting me, and that just wouldn't do. I can't have that.'

Bobo was slightly embarrassed about this, but quickly tried to brush it off. 'Oh, I didn't sleep with them, you know, I just hate being alone at night.'

Still, Unity wasn't overly discouraged by this little rejection. She kept thinking to herself how supremely excellent it would be to be 'the one' in Hitler's life, his one truly beloved partner in life, his wife. This desire was still strong. She also wanted to sleep with him and was perfectly willing, but could she lure Hitler to her bed? Could he ever be willing, or even able? So far, the most he'd ever done was shake her hand. Not even a kiss on the cheek yet. But of course she didn't take that to mean anything. *After all*, she thought, *he's really quite shy deep down, with a retiring demeanour, and too much of a gentleman to try anything more forward.*

It was obvious that Unity was totally in love (and lust) with Hitler. As soon as she saw him, she would get goosebumps, her gestures became animated, her face cheered up, and her eyes, glued to the man, radiated energy. Hitler was keeping it platonic, but the opportunity of a love relationship was there, if he ever chose to peruse it. Besides, what middle-aged man wouldn't have been flattered by the attentions of a high-born and pretty young woman like the adoring Unity Mitford?

What's more, she was different and a refreshing change from the other people around him. It wasn't only her foreign nationality that made her different. In the interests of being liked – or out of fear – the others always agreed with the Führer on everything or told him what they thought he wanted to hear: 'Yes, my Führer.' 'You're right, my Führer.' But Unity had never been that way with anyone. She was the only person in his inner circle who was not afraid to disagree with him and to debate the point, sometimes even with some insolence, stubbornness or force. It's a marvel that his fondness for her never faded. When someone criticised Unity for her manner, Hitler would even defend her: 'Her frankness is the British way.' And: 'How refreshing, a person who isn't scared to tell me what she really thinks!' Unity's innate rebel streak meant that she had always said and done as she pleased, and she saw herself in the example of Hitler, and so she would not and could not give up.

Unity was a quick-witted student and a fast learner of the language. Although she spoke German with a foreigner's accent, it was easy to understand her.

Unity was never boring to Hitler and certainly Hitler never bored her with his company. He enthralled her and she in turn was able to stimulate him with conversations about music, art, movies, books. She could also do gossip, and Hitler was big on gossip. But it was more than that – Unity was very intelligent, even intellectual. Hitler liked such women as friends, but as lovers or potential wives, they weren't his type. He liked to say that a man should always marry a sweet and stupid woman, one who wouldn't challenge his so-called mental superiority but who would be pleasant to be around. Nothing more was required, as far as the Führer was concerned. That's why he was attracted to the athletic beauty Eva Braun, who was all brawn and no brains.

Bobo ignored Eva and was very possessive and protective of the Führer. She once even had a fight over Hitler with her brother. 'Just for that, Tom, I won't introduce you to the Führer!' she said.

As soon as she got up in the morning at 11 a.m., as was her habit, Unity waited religiously by the telephone until at least 2 p.m. for Hitler to call and invite her for dinner at the Osteria or his private apartment. The tension of waiting for that call could be unbearable, but it was followed by the blissful climax of that telephone finally ringing, and the hour or two of bubbling anticipation while she got herself ready for him.

The car arrived for Unity and her sidekick Mary, and they were driven to Hitler's flat in the Prinzregentenstrasse.

Hitler was very hospitable and tried to make them feel most comfortable and at home. Knowing of Unity's sweet tooth, he offered her cream cakes.

'Oh, I really shouldn't,' said Bobo, 'I'm getting so fat!'

'Oh, have at least a nibble,' he insisted, 'I'll be disappointed if you don't.'

Hitler showed them a few new classical paintings he had bought, now hanging on the walls in the living room. 'Forget that degenerate modern art, there is no real art outside of the classics,' he firmly stated. 'I don't understand the preposterous popularity of alleged artists like Matisse or Picasso. This Picasso couldn't paint a Renaissance painting if his miserable life depended upon it, but I would bet you that Michelangelo had enough talent in his baby finger to paint any one of those ugly Cubist doodles with the greatest of ease. There's a very simple reason why the Dadaists and Cubists paint such trash – they paint as they do because they cannot paint.'

Unity nodded. 'The Impressionists and post-Impressionists were the last great artists,' she said.

'Yes. Admittedly, they broke the rules, but *they* could paint! The degenerate artists of today break the rules and *cannot* paint. There's a difference. Any slightly skilled art school student can imitate a Cubist painting quite impressively. That's not real talent.'

Hitler next took a globe atlas off the cabinet, spinning its axis. 'Look girls, I have the whole world in my hands,' he said with a laugh.

Unity was feeling great. Hitler was a good host, very polite and entertaining, she thought. He talked incessantly, about all the usual things he and Bobo liked discussing, but also education, politics, and other such heavy topics. He knew Unity could keep up with him on that level.

'Tell me about Winston Churchill and the Prince of Wales,' he remarked.

'Churchill is a drunken old troublemaker, no friend of yours, believe me. He takes every opportunity to criticise the Reich. Nobody likes him. But King Eddie is a dear old boy. It's a nice change to have a popular young new king like him, and he's very pro-Fascist, you know. You should meet him some day.'

'I hope I will,' said Hitler. 'By the way, you know the British monarchy has distinctly German roots.'

'Of course. But they're ashamed of those roots. They've uprooted them and replanted them on English Windsor soil.'

'Tell me more about your English monarchy. It seems such a relic of the past to have a monarchy, yet there's such a certain charm and splendour to all that is royal and regal.'

'Well there's nothing charming about our dull monarchy. Just a bunch of stiffs. And they hold no power today, you know. The royal family are only figureheads, only puppets of the government.

My family was once invited to Buckingham Palace. I brought along my pet rat and scared the bejesus out of everybody. It was great fun. Had to liven things up somehow...' She giggled.

After dinner, as they sat chatting over some glasses of wine, Unity yet again swerved the conversation towards the subject of marriage.

But the Führer was adamant. 'I have no time for marriage,' he reiterated. 'You see how I live, my dear. No woman could stand five minutes of this. My life and love I gave to Germany long ago.'

Hitler never tried to flirt with Unity in any way, and she felt slightly annoyed at this. It's because I'm fat and ugly, she convinced herself. He never flirted with Mary either. But his behaviour was easygoing and courteous and Unity sensed that she was important to him. It was the highlight of her existence just to indulge in these friendly occasions, however non-romantic they may be.

'Oh, before it slips my mind, I have something for you,' said Hitler, and he presented her with a gold party badge. This was even much more impressive than the party emblem she had received from the British Union of Fascists.

Receiving it threw her over the moon with excited glee. Her happiness could not be measured. Impulsively, she wrapped her arms around his neck and kissed him full on the cheek – she didn't dare go for the lips – and left him to wipe the lipstick off with a handkerchief. From that day forward, she was not capable of praising anyone but her beloved Führer.

Before they left, Hitler said, 'Oh, and I have another surprise for you.' He handed the pair another gift – a portrait painting of himself.

'I will treasure it forever and ever!' exclaimed Unity.

Unity was in the Osteria with Derek Hill, sitting at a table near the front entrance. It was noon-ish.

Derek had been back to England on a brief trip and he was chatting on, trying to interest her in some London gossip. But Bobo wasn't much interested. She hardly spoke.

'I say, am I boring you?' he asked.

'It would be better if you didn't say anything,' she answered. 'The Führer is coming. He doesn't know that I'm here already, so it will be a pleasant surprise for him.'

She was right. It wasn't long before the Nazi dictator and his whole procession flooded into the restaurant. It sent a shiver of excitement through Unity, as if she hadn't seen Hitler for weeks or months, even though she had been in his apartment with him just the evening before.

Hitler himself stopped at her table, bent over and muttered to her to join him, and then went off to rejoin his party.

Suddenly, Derek didn't exist for Unity, and she hurried off to be seated beside her idol. On the way over to his table, in her spellbound single-mindedness, she accidentally tripped – lanky, clumsy girl that she was – and her purse flew open, spilling out some of its contents – several toy guns.

Hitler's bodyguards immediately stood up and slung out their pistols, aiming them at a terrified Unity. But as soon as they picked up the toy guns and saw what they were, they laughed.

'What on earth do you have them for?' Hitler asked, shaking his head, bemused.

'They're for my son, after I have one,' she replied with a broad, toothy smile.

'Hm. I shall have to give you a *real* gun, a revolver… for self-defence,' he said.

'Oh yes, please do!' she replied.

Her wish was his command. She soon got it.

Unity invited her German teacher Fräulein Baum to meet Hitler at the Osteria. Hitler arrived and spent most of the time talking to Baum. Unity felt intensely jealous that the other woman was so singled out. Unity wanted to accuse her of being a Jew, she was so aflame with jealousy. Bobo soon found out that Baum was, in fact, a Jew. It was a shock. She stopped taking lessons with her.

Jessica came for a long-overdue visit and stayed with Unity. Unity talked unceasingly about Hitler, bragging about her friendship with him.

'What do you do when you don't see Hitler?' asked Jessica.

'I think of him.'

'And did Hitler give you the revolver?'

'As self-protection,' Unity explained. 'But also, if war is ever declared between Britain and Germany, then I'm prepared to shoot myself.'

'Is that his or your idea of self-protection?' said Jessica with sarcasm. 'You wouldn't be that foolish.'

'It would be foolish not to, since I wouldn't be able to stand seeing our two countries ripping each other to shreds with me caught in the middle. I wouldn't be able to bear it.'

'Well if you're fool enough to follow Hitler, who knows what you're capable of? I've heard that Hitler's horoscope warns of catastrophes, collapse, and death by his own hand.'

'Oh that damn astrology. You can never believe in it. Half of it ends up happening and the other half doesn't. It's not reliable. Did I tell you I'm going to become a German citizen?'

'Oh, don't be such a fool,' said Jessica. 'Next thing you'll be telling me that you've renounced your British citizenship.'

Julius Streicher, a prominent anti-Jewish agitator and close friend of Hitler, was not in the Nazi military, but he was the most well-known spreader of anti-Semitic propaganda in the Third Reich.

He owned and ran a very popular high-circulation newspaper, *Der Stürmer*, which he used as the vehicle of his violent and rabid views. The newspaper went on and on about Jews, using the age-old anti-Semitic stereotypes, lies and exaggerations. These ideas had long been ingrained in Unity's mind, since she had been reading it religiously for years.

A forced Jewish exodus to Siberia just isn't an option now in 1936, as Russia doesn't yet belong to the Reich, she pondered. *It will be cheaper and easier to just burn them all here. Burn the Jews, that's the thing for them. We'll turn it into a fashionable pastime. Parents will take their kids on Sunday to watch the bonfire of the Jews.*

Unity hit it off with Streicher right from the start when he overwhelmed her with a flower bouquet at one of Hitler's outdoor table-talk get-togethers. Realising how slim her chances were with Hitler, Unity started to interest herself in Streicher. They became close, flirting with each other. She showed Streicher kind attention in front of Hitler, trying to make the Führer jealous. She never forgot how ignored she felt that time she had brought along Baum and Hitler had talked to her the whole time, ignoring Unity.

Streicher took Unity to his private office and offered her a drink. He was a chronically insecure little man with a bald head and beefy frame. Some likened him to a pig. Others said he was not very intelligent. But unlike Hitler, who was intelligent, Streicher looked up to and admired women of breeding, culture, and intellect.

'You're an impressive young woman, Unity Mitford,' he said, sipping his champagne and giving her a wink. 'A woman with gifts. I would bet that you are highly educated, aren't you?'

'Well, I used to draw pictures of nudes, and they kicked me out of school,' she said matter-of-factly.

Streicher chuckled and took out a portfolio, spreading it open and showing her photographs of naked girls he had taken. 'These are girls who admitted to me that they slept with Jews. But they repented in good time and are now my mistresses.'

'Aren't you afraid of catching some venereal disease or something from them? After all, they had polluted their bodies.'

'Unlike Jews, who are the spreaders of every disease known to man,' said Streicher stupidly, 'the only illness I've ever known is nympholepsy.'

'What's that?'

'Compulsive sexual desire for something or someone unattainable.'

'Well I have that too!' cried Unity. 'Ever since I fell for the Führer.'

'With me it's Jewesses,' admitted Streicher. 'I want to sleep with them, but committing such an abomination would bring me to the brink of suicide. I can allow myself only the fantasy of it. But that's enough for me. You see, I have a very vivid imagination.' He said this with a lewd grin.

'But why would you want to sleep with a Jewess!' snapped Unity.

He paused and smiled. 'You know the universal saying? "Forbidden fruit tastes the best."'

He slithered up to Unity and wrapped his arms around her shoulders in a tight, warm clasp. Unity saw the glint in his eye. He looked sexually aroused. 'You know, this whole Nazi thing is such great fun,' he breathed into her ear. 'You are such great fun. You don't know how sexy and irresistible you look strutting around Central Europe in your blackshirts uniform and sporting a gun. The first time I laid eyes on you was at an evening torchlight party procession. You looked like a Nordic moon goddess or something. So, so beautiful…'

'If I were a god or goddess,' said Unity, 'I would unite all the Nordic countries as one with Britain… But just you wait, sooner or later *everyone* will be fascist.'

Unity went to spend a long weekend with Mary and her family at their cottage on Hayling Island, off the south coast of England, as a summer holiday.

When she arrived she knocked on the door. Mary's father answered it and received her. 'Hello, do come in,' he said. 'I'm afraid everyone has gone out sailing. But do make yourself at home. They should be back by dinner time. If I can offer you anything, do let me know.' He disappeared to do some work at his desk in another room.

Oh dear, I wish I had brought along a book to read, thought Unity, slouching down in an armchair.

A quarter of an hour later, Bobo was outside with her revolver, shooting at a thick pine tree that she had chosen as a target.

Mary's father came running out of the cottage. 'What the devil are you doing?'

'Just a little target practice.'

'Why?'

'I'm practising to kill Jews.'

He asked her to leave on the spot.

Unity's status within Hitler's inner circle was on the rise. It was unbelievable but true that she was a frequent private guest of the most powerful man in Central Europe, and often seen publicly as a close companion of his. Everyone saw this and it made an impression. Consequently, this meant that many people of importance wished to be acquainted with her as well. They all showered her with invitations and paid her fares and tickets, since sooner or later she would come in useful. Somehow or other she never seemed to go away for very long. Her trips back to England became fewer and briefer. She couldn't bear being separated from her cherished and treasured Führer.

Men were attracted to her and were full of flirtation and compliments, but women often envied her. They were nice to her face, yet stabbed her in the back as soon as it was turned. Unity, however, would make them pay. While with Streicher at a party, she made fun of the women: 'How frumpy they look, how dreadfully plain, these housewives of senior Nazi officials. Most of them don't even wear make-up or style their hair properly. And those old-fashioned granny clothes from 1910 or something. I wouldn't be caught dead in a dress like that!'

Streicher laughed. 'You're behaving as though this party were an operetta or beauty contest. The Führer likes his women to look like that. He's rather old-fashioned himself, you know.'

Now that she felt her German was good enough and she was no longer with Baum, Unity enrolled at the Technische Hochschule and started taking lessons in mathematics under Professor Honigschmitt.

'You're a good student, a fast learner!' said the kind and benevolent professor after Unity completed a difficult mathematical equation at the blackboard.

Next she wanted professional vocal lessons and became the private pupil of a once-famous (although now retired) tenor, whose wife was in fact a granddaughter of the composer Grieg. Unity sang him an aria while he accompanied her on piano.

'You have a wonderful voice!' he enthused at the end of the song, assuring her that she was born to sing the part of Elsa in the Wagner opera *Lohengrin*. For Unity, that would have been another dream come true.

But she was the type who could always find something to be down about, even in a moment of triumph. She was haunted by a feeling of never being good enough. 'Sure I can sing and dance and draw,' she muttered, 'but if I could only write! You see, all my sisters are terribly talented writers, and so I've always felt left out among them. I could read a novel very well all right, but I could never come close to writing one, like my older sister Nancy. She's a famous novelist, you see.'

There were times, Unity realised, that she felt deeply unhappy. She had never known real love, not even within her own family, and therefore didn't always know how to give it. That was what made it easy for her to hate the Jews. Even her father, the one person who truly loved her, was not the sort of man to often show his love, kind and mild-mannered though he was. He was just too mellow. He was capable of moments of affection, but they were few and far between. Bobo was a wounded creature with an inferiority complex in her family, always looking for a place to fit in, to make herself valued. She had found this in Hitler and Nazism. She felt she had found somewhere where she could finally belong.

As someone who was invited to all the most fashionable gatherings, Unity went to a dinner party hosted at the house of Munich's most celebrated couple, Lali and Freddy Horstmann.

During dinner, Prince Lippe-Biesterfeld fearlessly belittled Hitler, condemning the Nazis.

Unity gave him a harsh frown but listened in silence and didn't say a word, as if she had something up her sleeve. *You will never speak that way again*, she thought to herself.

Sure enough, two days later the prince was arrested in his home and taken away, with his wife and kids pleading for mercy, knowing that they would never see him again.

One really needed to be careful what one did or said around Unity. She was powerful and dangerous. Certain people observed this and kept away from her. If you were denounced by Unity as anti-Nazi, the mere accusation would mean that you ended up in a concentration camp.

A person could never be sure of remaining in Unity's good graces, even if he were the quintessential Aryan. Unity was nice and flirty with Helmut, a young blonde German in a black Nazi uniform, but as soon as she sensed that he showed no interest in meeting Hitler, she became dismissive, bored, and even furious with him. A dislike or indifference towards her Hitler was, to her mind, the most terrible thing imaginable. If her worship of Hitler had been a religion, this would have amounted to blasphemy or sacrilege of the worst kind. She contrived never to see Helmut again.

Diana was sent from England by Oswald Mosley to procure the financial support of the Nazis for the British Union of Fascists. Mosley could not do this directly, for fear of the political damage it could do to him at home, so he sent his mistress on his behalf.

She was standing with Unity before a row of guards near the doors of the gigantic and spacious entrance lobby of a grand hotel. Hitler was scheduled to arrive and Unity wanted him to see her and her sister immediately upon his arrival.

Ten minutes later, the Führer's car drove in and Hitler strode into the entrance lobby, looking stern and formal. Upon being greeted by everyone inside with a shout of 'Heil!' he instinctively put his hand up in salute. Suddenly, his eyes met Unity's and immediately his expression softened and his face lit up with a beaming smile.

'My dear Unity! You must come and have tea with us!'

Hitler was extremely jovial, polite and flattering, dubbing Unity and Diana 'perfect specimens of Aryan womanhood'.

'I will do what I can for your Mosley,' said Hitler, giving Diana some important contacts and assuring her that funds would be forthcoming.

Overall, Hitler admired the British; but it was not all praise. Diana didn't speak any German, so Hitler was able to make disparaging remarks about the British in her company without offending. As a private joke, Unity gave her sister a totally false translation of what he was saying and Diana nodded and smiled at Hitler the whole time, unknowing.

Streicher walked by and Unity waved to him enthusiastically. 'He brings me flowers and is a wonderful flirt. He's a true darling,' she said to Diana.

That evening there was a huge party at the Chancellery and Unity found herself in one of her lively discussions with her Führer. It was generally of a jocular, teasing kind. Hitler loved to entertain with impressions of various people, including himself. He imitated Oswald Mosley during one of his speeches, and the joke was that Mosley imitated Hitler's oratory theatrics and mannerisms to a T, so an imitation of Mosley was really an imitation of himself. He made jokes about Unity wearing too much make-up: 'You don't need to paint yourself so much, you're not an actress and I don't believe that you're a prostitute – as far as I know, anyway. You don't sleep with my officers for pay.' He also made a giraffe joke about her being too tall.

In return, Unity dared to make light-hearted jokes about Hitler having no sex life – nothing too cruel, just light banter, which didn't offend Hitler. As a dedicated reader of Streicher's anti-Semitic newspaper, she also revealed herself to be very fond of pornographic Yiddish jokes.

Many of those who heard her conversation looked shocked and even appalled. Unity could not help but notice. 'As you well know, my Führer, I'm not afraid to say anything, anything I please. I always think aloud.'

Hitler joked, 'Indeed, you talk so much that whenever I have anything to announce to the world, I have only to tell *you*.'

That remark induced a roar of laughter from the table.

The German national anthem started playing and Unity was indignant that the people at the party didn't stop dancing. 'They don't know how to show proper reverence and respect,' she complained.

But to Hitler she was apparently overreacting. 'Maybe the dancing itself is their expression of nationalism,' was the

Führer's retort. 'Perhaps they deserve your praise rather than condemnation,' he said in a slyly ironic way.

'They deserve a swift kick in the buttocks,' she stubbornly stated, and her fanaticism would not be swayed by the party atmosphere.

In spring 1936, Unity set off and joined her mother and sisters on a Mediterranean cruise to Gibraltar, Algiers, Athens, even Istanbul.

On the return trip, they stopped at a southern port in Spain to see the Alhambra. Unity was wearing the gold swastika badge with Hitler's signature engraved on the back. It was her statement of allegiance to dictatorship.

An infuriated radical left-wing Spaniard came up to Unity in Granada and within a few moments she was surrounded by a swarming mob. They clawed at her blouse, tearing at the despised symbol.

Luckily for Unity, this was near the port, and cruise personnel from the ship leaped into the crowd and bulldozed through, rescuing her and hurrying her back aboard to safety.

Unity and her mother had a heated exchange about the swastika, which escalated into a hair-pulling fiasco. Unity was saved again, this time from her mother, and escorted into her private cabin.

At dinner, among her mother and sisters and other guests, Unity stood up and proposed a toast to the Führer.

Her mother said aloud to all assembled: 'I'm normal, my husband is normal, but my daughters are each one more foolish than the other. What do you say about my daughter Unity? Isn't it very sad?'

At the Nuremberg Rally, Hitler arranged it so that Unity was seated beside his rumoured mistress, Eva Braun. Unity, among many others, didn't believe that there was anything much going on between them. He had, after all, assured her that his only real mistress was Germany. Still, both Unity and Eva were bitterly jealous of each other over Hitler, and competed for his affections and attention. Unity didn't like this one little bit, and she asked the girl sitting behind her to trade seats.

That night, resentful of the rumours about Hitler and Eva, Unity wrote to her sister Diana, 'She is known as a simple country bumpkin, and she looks like the typical dairy-maid, except for her small breasts, but she has ugly legs, which a few blind people have called beautiful. She's tall like me but her body has no shape. I know the Führer likes women with curves better. I have nice curves. Really, what the greatest man in Germany sees in her, I do not know. I sit here by the telephone, waiting for his call while his absence mocks me.'

Then she folded her letter and sealed it in an envelope, ready to send off. She crossed her arms and in a pouting expression said aloud to Mary, 'Who is this Eva Braun bitch? She isn't even a real blonde like me. What does she have that I don't? How does she do it? You must have noticed that he doesn't invite me to his private flat anymore – no doubt because *she's* there.'

Unity was shortly afterwards secretly informed by an ally in the Hitler circle that Eva Braun instructed Hitler's cronies to never allow Unity to be alone with him. This so infuriated Unity that she took out her gun and thought about shooting and murdering Eva. But when she calmed down, she thought better of it and put the gun back in the drawer.

Two weeks later, Unity learned of how Eva had tried to commit suicide by overdosing on sleeping pills. Hitler was deeply shaken and made himself much more attentive to her emotional needs, even going so far as to put her up in a grand villa with a maid, a cook, and a Mercedes.

This made Unity seethe. But it taught her an important lesson: to maintain the Führer's interest, she might have to act out in a terribly desperate and dramatic way, too.

At a party of the Anglo-German League, Lady Redesdale, attending the event with her daughter, mentioned to Putzi Hanfstaegl, 'You must not under any circumstances say anything about your Führer, or my daughter Unity will spoil everyone's evening with her Hitler talk.'

Although Putzi did not start it, the subject of Hitler inevitably came up, and Unity immediately leaped from her chair and waxed on and on about how wonderful Hitler was and how well she knew him.

Putzi appeared quite irritated. 'Who the hell are you and who the hell do you think you are talking like that?'

She boldly answered, 'Don't you realise? I am Unity Mitford.'

The room, crowded with people, was suddenly quiet, so Putzi broke the silence by making critical remarks about 'the crazy militarisation and soldier-cult of the Nazi party'.

'If you think this, you have no right to go on being Hitler's foreign press chief!' spat Unity.

He ignored the outburst. 'You know, Miss Mitford,' he said, 'you may be *persona grata* with Hitler and his crowd, but you're not meant for politics. You know nothing about it. According to Nazi social expectations, girls like you are meant for seducing a man and popping out a bunch of children – though you still have none, and I don't know whether you ever went to bed with anyone.'

'What a funny little nitwit you are…' Unity smirked.

'You know, Unity, you Hitler-loving girls, the way you maidens stretch your arms out in Nazi salute fifty times a day, it must cause muscle and joint pain in the arms. How do you manage it so consistently without going to massage therapy?' he said, mockingly.

'Drop dead!'

'You think you're so important to Hitler. I would bet you never stop talking about your so-called friendship with him, but Hitler's never even mentioned you to me. You could just as well be another nameless devotee, for all he cares. He told me, 'The crowd is a woman and has sexual appeal, and after a speech I feel as if I have had sexual release.' The Führer's only mistress is the German woman, every German woman. He's fond of saying that he cannot ever marry just one, or else all the others would fall out of love with him.'

'Oh thanks for telling me, as if I didn't know that already, you dunce,' said Unity with a wry and menacing grimace, shaking her head.

Unity's father bought her a shiny black MG sports car with a back seat and room for several passengers.

'It's lovely!' she enthused.

She realised that now she would not have to rely on public transport and had complete freedom of movement, which most women did not yet enjoy. Unity decorated it with swastika flags and a long Nazi banner.

She was seized by a mania for speed and travel, a wanderlust. But when Mary made a joke by calling her 'the Wandering Jew', Bobo almost slapped her in the face.

'Not funny!' cried Unity.

Unity now drove all over Germany in her brand new car, and it was a matter of supreme indifference to her if she happened to park somewhere illegally. The only rules she deigned to follow were her own. She looked cool and very well-dressed – obviously someone from a wealthy, affluent, leisure-class background. The back seat was full of her stuff, an untidy assortment of books and gramophone records. She also took along her German dictionary anywhere she went. Although she had quickly picked up the language and thought she spoke it fairly well for a foreigner, she had only been speaking it for a few years and knew that there was a lot of room for improvement.

Unity burst into her flat. Jessica was there. She had been let in by Bobo's room-mate Mary and was staying with them during the Winter Olympics, which were going to be hosted in Germany that year.

'Hi Jessica! Glad you made it.'

'Glad to be here,' replied Jessica.

'I'm so sorry, I wish I could stay, but I have the entire government waiting outside.'

'What do you mean? I don't believe you,' said Jessica with a little laugh. She went to the window and saw that Unity was telling the truth.

'Oh God,' sighed Jessica.

Unity giggled, grabbed Mary by the elbow, and ran to the front door, shouting back at Jessica, 'In the meantime, make yourself at home. I'll be back tonight…' Unity and Mary disappeared into the car at the front, in which Goebbels and his wife were already seated.

They arrived at a roaring party – full of good-looking SS officers in uniform, Unity was pleased to observe. *Oh, how strong, sharp, and handsome a man can look in uniform*, she mused. People were becoming very festive and tipsy, in some cases drunk. Ties were loosened, women let their hair down, and many bottles were opened.

The party ended at about two in the morning, but Unity had still not had enough. She and a band of others found their way to an all-night café. Unity jumped up on a trestle table in her camel-hair coat and tried to do a striptease, encouraged by the bartender, but the proprietor quickly put an end to it and none-too-gently pulled Bobo down.

'Don't touch me or I'll tell the Führer!' threatened a half-drunk Unity.

'You don't like to be touched? Or maybe just by the Führer?' said the bartender to her with a grin.

She sat down at the bar of the café opposite him and muttered, 'The happiest moment of my life was sitting at his feet and him stroking my hair…'

The bartender smiled at her incredulously and gave her another gin and tonic.

The next day, Unity was overjoyed to hear that Jessica was pregnant. She had been married just under a year ago.

'So it must have been conceived on your honeymoon,' said Bobo with a wink. 'Anyway, I talked to the Führer over the telephone earlier and told him that my sister was visiting, so he's invited us to dine with him this evening. You know he met and loved Diana, but he simply adores pregnant women, so you know he'll adore you. He loves to put his hand on the stomach and feel the infant kicking.'

'Well, I don't like the idea of that,' said Jessica. 'I'm afraid I can't allow it. Besides, the baby is still very small.' Jessica was of course a communist, and so had no particular liking for the fascist dictator.

Unity went to have a bath to make herself 'presentable' for dinner with the Führer, and the telephone rang.

'Can you grab that please?' hollered Unity, soaking in the tub.

Jessica picked it up but the man on the other line started speaking German and Jessica didn't understand, so she placed the telephone back on the hook.

'Who was it?' asked Unity when she came out, wrapped in a towel.

'Don't know. Couldn't understand a word. All I can remember is the word "Julius".'

'That was probably my sweetheart Julius Streicher. How could you be so nasty to darling Streicher?'

'What does he look like?' asked Jessica.

Unity showed her a framed photograph Streicher had given her.

Jessica sneered. 'He doesn't look very darling to me, more like a disgusting little man with no hair.'

'Take that back! I think he's very handsome.'

'Think as you like,' said Jessica.

'What about the Führer then? Have you ever seen his marvellous blue eyes?' Bobo asked in an effusion of emotion.

'No, but I've heard he has hideous, cruel steely-grey eyes. Haven't you?' her sister retorted with a very sarcastic sense of humour.

'Oh, shut up with your nonsense,' Unity muttered. She reached into her purse and pulled out a small, pearl-handled pistol. 'This is to defend myself with against attacks from Jews, communists or whoever. So don't infuriate me.'

'Would you really contemplate persecuting and torturing a Jew?'

Unity avoided answering the question directly, saying only, 'Streicher says they're so wicked.'

They happily changed the subject and started talking about marriage and motherhood. Unity made a shocking statement: 'I plan to have eight darling little bastards, all with different fathers.'

'Oh, nice…' said the sarcastic, pregnant and happily married Jessica, rolling her eyes at Unity.

The summer of 1937 was so hot in Munich that Unity went out and found a really secluded little spot in the Englischer Garten, a very large park located in the centre of Munich.

She found a very quiet and lonely place, rather hidden away. Exhibitionist that she was, Unity took all her clothes off so that she could attain an all-body tan. Even her swimsuit came off. It did cross her mind that sooner or later she might be seen; however, luckily for her, no one came along to think her mad as well as indecent.

After the suntanning, she met Magda Goebbels in town to go shopping. She and Magda were becoming close friends.

'I'm going to buy a new dress today,' said Unity. She held Hitler's portrait under her arm, the one he had given her. It was in a silver frame. 'I'll have this put in a nicer frame as well, a new gold frame,' she added. The back of the canvas was signed:

For Unity Mitford, as a reminder of our friendship, Adolf Hitler.

She carried it in the street uncovered, for all to see. This was just like Unity. Provocative.

After buying their clothes, Magda suggested that they sit outdoors at a bistro and have some early dinner. Unity rested her portrait against the leg of the table, in open view of all in the street. Unity could see that this made even fanatical Nazi Magda a little uneasy, but that didn't bother her in the least.

Several days later, Bobo took Magda to visit England with her. Lord Redesdale was waiting for them at Victoria Station and escorted them back to the family abode, Swinbrook House.

Unity gave Magda a tour of the mansion.

'It's haunted, you know. Every once in a while, a ghost pops up somewhere.'

This seemed to frighten Magda.

'Just joking!' Unity laughed.

'It's not very funny, actually,' said Magda. 'I've lived in China, where ghosts and spirits are very much a part of life.'

Darkness fell and they retired to bed, but minutes later Magda sneaked into Unity's bedroom, which was right next to hers, and whispered, 'I heard some strange noises.'

'You can sleep with me if you like,' offered Unity.

Magda snuggled up under the covers and brought them up to her chin, rubbing up against Unity. Bobo could feel her trembling slightly, which made her chuckle to herself.

The door opened without a knock the following morning and a short, fat maid came in to put an English breakfast of bacon and eggs on a tray beside the bed. She didn't speak a word and quietly left, almost as quickly as she had come in.

Minutes passed and then there came a terrible banging from outside.

'What's that?' asked Magda.

'Oh, that's probably just Sir Oswald shooting a hare for our supper,' said Unity, turning over to face her while stretching and yawning.

With Unity as guide, they set out to explore Oxford and to visit at Diana's house. Unity sat behind the wheel and the two of them sang German songs. It was hard to tell which one of them knew more Nazi songs. Incidentally, both of them were avid readers and had read *Mein Kampf* dozens of times.

'Magda, tell me, what does the Führer really think of me?'

Magda seemed slightly evasive. 'You know, he loves the company of young women like you, and with you he's the same as with any other pretty girl – politeness itself.'

Unity felt that she was downplaying her significance in Hitler's life. 'But do you think that's all I am to him? Just another girl? That can't be so.'

'The Führer has spoken to my husband about you, saying how typically British you are – far too fanatical. But don't take it the wrong way, he's very pleased with you. He says you started out as a simple admirer, a dedicated enthusiast, and have evolved into a sophisticated and useful propagandist. Overall, he is very glad to have you around. You're his ideal; he loves tall blonde women, and not too slim, those with a little more meat on their bones. Eva Braun is very jealous; she's jealous of everybody that keeps her away from a leader who she fancies, more importantly, as her lover.'

'I will never believe that he is her lover, never. I would never believe that my Führer would lie to me like that. As far as my propaganda goes, I'm only too happy to send letters to *Der Stürmer* about the "Jewish danger" and have them published.'

Nevertheless, even with Unity's obvious loyalty to the Nazi cause, Magda explained to Unity that many in Hitler's circle continued to warn him about her. To them, she was an enigma – a puzzle they couldn't quite piece together.

Magda told Unity that behind her back they asked, 'What is this Unity Mitford after, really? Is she in the pay of the British secret service, maybe through her uncle Winston Churchill himself? Or can she genuinely be such a huge fan of the Führer as she claims, such a steadfast supporter of the Nazis?'

It was plain that such suspicions were upsetting to Unity's ears. Not what she wanted to hear.

In her defence, Magda said, 'But Hitler brushes it off, convinced of your authenticity, that you're deeply and truly devoted to him and his cause, indeed too much so.'

'I know! In fact, the Führer takes me into his confidence and delights in divulging to me any number of guarded political and military secrets,' Bobo boasted. 'If he thought I was a fraud or a spy, he would never do this. So he knows I am for real.'

Magda reasoned, 'He tells you certain secrets because he hopes that you'll convey them elsewhere, namely to the British government. But he's very careful and selective about what he says around you. Of course, there's also a lot of this kind of information that he doesn't want you to know and tell, top-secret stuff that he simply doesn't want his enemies to have and that he doesn't discuss either with you or in front of you.'

'Well, I would never do anything to harm Hitler or the Reich,' said Unity. 'Such information is safe with me. Mum's the word.' She said this without realising her reputation for being a blabbermouth who could never keep anything to herself.

'I've never believed for a second that you're a secret agent. But it does seem incredible to me how you always seem to know Hitler's timetable and everything about his daily life, not only his political doings but also his personal life.'

Bobo laughed. 'That's true!'

'My husband told me about the time the Führer was scheduled for afternoon tea at the famous art museum in Munich and, wouldn't you know it, you were already there waiting for him just five minutes ahead of him.'

Unity laughed again even louder. 'The Führer was flabbergasted. "How on earth did you know I would be here?" he gasped.'

'What did you say?' asked Magda.

'I told him, "I have my sources."'

They grinned at each other.

A Labour politician was giving a party speech in Hyde Park. Dressed in her blackshirts uniform as usual and sporting her swastika broach, Bobo was in attendance at the edge of the crowd.

A bold young communist standing beside her turned to her and suddenly ripped the swastika broach off of her, violently tossing it to the ground. Incredible. It felt like the incident in Spain all over again. *Déjà vu*. A furious Unity slapped him across the face.

The crowd around her was certainly not a fascist-friendly crowd, and Unity soon felt their hostility towards her. They started shouting insults at her. A woman said something insulting about Hitler and told Unity, 'Go back to Germany!' Unity punched her square in the face, knocking her over.

The crowd didn't give Unity a chance to retrieve the broach and surrounded her from all sides, but her defiant anger made her brave and she didn't feel any great fear or panic. Quickly she was besieged by a hoard of people shoving her and crying further insults and threats.

'I'll duck you in the Serpentine!' said one.

'Let's hang her from a tree!' proposed another.

They seized her kicking and screaming, and started dragging her away. A number of police officers appeared and cleared the space around Unity, safely escorting her away. But the crowd didn't give up, and kept up a pursuit, stalking her towards Park Lane.

By then the crowd had worked itself up in a frenzy and were chanting 'Kill!' No longer were they just hurling insults; they were hurling stones.

Lucky for Unity, there was a bus stop ahead and a bus had just pulled up. She and the policemen hopped aboard.

Some of the demonstrators tried to board the bus, but the policemen stood by the door to prevent them.

Unity took a comfortable seat and gazed out the bus window, feeling relieved. For the first time, her eyes were confronted by the full magnitude of the raging crowd outside, at least 300 people.

One of the police officers approached. 'Are you all right, miss? Not injured?'

'Not at all,' said Unity. 'Not in the least. And I was not really frightened, only stirred up,' she added nonchalantly.

However, if it hadn't been for the police protection and, in effect, rescue, there would have been no telling what might have happened to her at the mercy of the mob. It could have ended in drowning or lynching.

The newspapers took the sensational story and ran with it, milking it for all it was worth. Unity remained casual, fearless and defiant.

'You can say about me from this incident,' she said to one reporter for *The Daily Telegraph*, 'that the courage of my convictions is certainly not in question.' Then she turned languidly sad and glum. 'But my gold broach was trampled underfoot, and

I'm afraid I've lost it for good. I don't think it can be said that I did anything to provoke or irritate. Still, I regret the whole thing happened. The Führer does not mind men getting into fights, but he doesn't like women getting into them as he thinks it undignified. I'm afraid he may be cross with me for becoming so conspicuous for the cause.'

Hitler wanted very much to have faith in the fervent idealism of his number-one fan and her ability to bring their two mighty nations together in peaceful alliance. He never allowed anyone to throw the rotten tomatoes of criticism at her. It was a popular subject for the press. A cartoon and a funny little ditty were even printed about it:

> You can't criticise Unity
> with impunity.
> If you try to belittle her,
> you'll have to answer to Hitler.

Diana Mosley travelled back to Germany with younger sister Unity and newfound friend Magda. Shockingly, she had divorced her husband and married her lover, Oswald Mosley.

Hitler received her most graciously, with his usual emphasis on courtesy, which he exercised on all beautiful Aryan women. They all took to their seats for lunch. Hermann Göring, commander-in-chief of the Luftwaffe, was in attendance.

As soon as Diana started praising her husband and talking enthusiastically about the progress of the British fascist movement under his leadership, and about anti-Semitism being on the rise, Hitler abruptly and curtly cut her off.

'No, fascism doesn't lie in the English character,' he said. 'It's too alien to your nationality, and the English have not embraced it enough. Your Mosley may be a fine man, a man with ability, with an understanding of the weaknesses and failures of democratic government and a keen agenda for reform, but he cannot seduce an entire nation so overrun by immigrants who are so set on fighting and damaging him and who are so democratically protected.'

Unity the propagandist suddenly turned spy and informant, and blabbed endlessly about how weak and shoddy Great Britain's armoured defences were, about there being only a handful of anti-aircraft guns in all, a lack of up-to-date equipment and weaponry, and only two functional armoured divisions ready to defend its native island in the event of one of Hitler's devastating *blitzkrieg* attacks. Yes indeed, the army was a sorry sight.

Hitler was startled by these comments, this news, and listened most attentively, which thrilled Unity. Nothing pleased her more than to see him as putty in her hands.

'But the navy is a fine navy, with a legendary reputation going back centuries. The air force is also strong and ready, or so I hear.'

Göring scoffed at this last remark, raising his voice: 'They are no match for my fighter planes. German engineering cannot be beat. We'll chew them up and spit them out! The whole so-called British air *farce* will be blown out of the sky in a flash. Remember these words…!'

Unity's old crush Albert came to visit her in Munich.

'You're still the pretty, child-like pussycat of old,' he said teasingly, grinning.

He had seen her last as an eighteen-year-old deb. Her face had changed little in the last five years, although her body had become fuller, more buxom and womanly at the age of twenty-three.

'You forgot to mention I'm much fatter now,' she self-deprecatingly sighed.

'No, not fat. You no longer have the body of a teen, but a real woman, that's all. You're so tall, and full-figured, and beautiful... So much sex appeal. You've always been the best-looking to me.'

She gently brushed his cheek with the back of her hand. 'Oh Al, you always were the sweetest...' She said this with a typically expressionless face, but was clearly touched.

When she sat down at the Osteria opposite Al, she held her hand loosely folded over her lap, to cover what she believed was a slightly chubby tummy, as women sometimes do when photographs are taken.

'I wonder if the Führer will come today,' she said.

'What will you have?' asked Al, as if ignoring the remark.

'Oh nothing for me, thanks. The plump piglet has had enough for today. Don't even ask me how many chocolate éclairs I ate earlier. I'm bad.'

'Oh, please stop about the weight,' said Al, smiling.

'The Führer has a weak spot for chocolate éclairs too,' she added.

Al started teasing her about her well-known hero-worship of Hitler, which she didn't like at all, so he simply asked, 'What's he really like anyway?'

'He has marvellous, intense and penetrating eyes, silky hair, and is utterly wonderful. I always feel safe with him around. He's my lord and saviour, like Jesus Christ.'

'Do you mean that literally?'

'Well, let me put it this way. I was at Diana's recently for a few days with the wife of the German Minister of Propaganda. There had been a wild storm raging outside all night. At breakfast the following morning they all asked me, "Weren't you frightened last night? Lightning struck the tree outside your window." "Yes, I was scared," I told them, "but then I took the Führer's photograph to bed with me and I felt quite safe again."'

Al nodded and chuckled through a beaming smile. Bobo could see that he didn't understand her devotion; he must have found it amusing, something to snicker at.

Unity was still fond of Al, but she realised that she could not love him, because the essential ingredient was missing – he did not share her belief in Hitler. Moreover, it was this idolatry of Hitler that had always prevented her from giving herself to another man, since all her love went to her idol. She was happy to indulge in friendship and sex with people of her choosing, but her heart and soul belonged to the Führer, always – and this in spite of the fact that Hitler had turned her down.

She couldn't have Hitler; he was not available. She had fixed her sights on him, but it was not to be. There were so many things standing in their way – Hitler's jealous cronies, his intimate inhibitions, his megalomaniacal ambitions – not to mention another girl, Eva Braun. It was hopeless. She felt so frustrated and depressed. What could she do about it?

She tried to find comfort in the arms of another man and decided to fuck the dashingly good-looking and blonde Stabschef Viktor Lutze, who was the leader of the SA. Lutze had lost an eye in battle and wore a fake glass eye in its place, but Unity thought him very attractive in spite of it.

He popped the eye out before they did the deed, which Unity found amusing, but when it was over she felt guilty, as if she were betraying Hitler. Of course, she had no deep feelings for Lutze – but still.

At lunch with Hitler the very next day, Unity kept her eyes averted the whole time and was quite reticent. She was terrified, imagining over and over to herself, *The Führer will be able to read it in my eyes*.

Unity told this story to Al. She didn't care what he might say. As she expected, he started making jokes.

'You shouldn't make fun of his pop-out eyeball,' Unity spat. 'At least he doesn't have a great big nose like you!'

'You, for instance, never show your teeth when you smile because they're crooked,' he shot back.

'They are not!'

'And you'll soon have tonsillitis from the strain you put on your vocal chords shouting "Heil Hitler!"'

'You're horrid!' she exclaimed.

He laughed. 'Oh, don't get upset, just teasing.'

'Just don't tease me about my weight or I'll scratch your eyes out like the pussycat you say I am.'

'Yes, ma'am,' he said with a slight chuckle and smile.

Unity could be full of humour, but laughable as well, prattling on and on that she might have to commit suicide one day.

'If you did, where would you shoot yourself?' Al asked. 'What part of the body?'

'The head.' She pulled her handgun from out of her purse to show him.

Al looked it over in his hands for a moment, and replied, 'Such a silly little pistol as you have just will not do. And besides, bullets fired at the temple can easily deflect off the skull.'

'Well I doubt it. My skull surely can't be nearly as thick as yours,' said Unity, sticking her tongue out at him.

France and Britain had signed a treaty that promised to protect and defend Czechoslovakia if Germany were to attack it. But the Prime Minister Neville Chamberlain and other high-ranking conservative politicians in his cabinet, including the Earl of Halifax, were more interested in appeasement of Hitler to avoid another Great War. They were secretly willing to sacrifice the tiny Czech state if it meant peace. But if they thought that Hitler would go no further, they were sorely mistaken. What they failed to realise was that Hitler was bent on conquest of the whole of Europe. Britain's weak and timid stance gave him the courage to strongly and boldly defy the treaty.

Magda Goebbels ran to Unity, informing her of the news. 'Hitler says he's going to pulverise the Czechs into submission before the year is through. His chiefs of staff are getting ready for an aggressive attack.'

That instant, burning inside with adrenalin and excitement, Unity felt as if she had been ordered by Hitler to hop in her car and make her way to Prague. Feeling herself to be exceedingly important to Hitler, she considered herself his arch propagandist, like a female version of Goebbels, and immediately saw it as her role to beef up support for Hitler among the Czechs, especially German Czechs, many of whom lived along the border of Czechoslovakia and were known as Sudetens.

She entered Czechoslovakia on her British passport and made her way down to the Czech capital of Prague. She checked into the elegant Esplanade Hotel, a meeting place for the cultural, business, and political elite located in the heart of Prague, across from the State Opera.

Tall and blonde and arrogant, Unity strode into the hotel lobby, a new yet equally provocative swastika badge in her buttonhole. She saw how the hotel manager behind the front desk frowned at her swastika.

Her first words were, 'They booted me out of London for wearing it, but I'd like to see you try it here.'

She took a suite for the night, briskly snatching the room key from the manager's hand and stomping off.

The following morning she had a rendezvous with Sudeten German Senator Wollner, and they both got in her car to drive to the famous Czech spa of Karlove Vary, or Carlsbad, as it's known in German. Bobo knew she had a tough propaganda campaign ahead of her, and she wanted to make sure that she felt healthy and relaxed beforehand. It was on this pretext that she planned to visit the spa. And besides, what rich girl doesn't like to be pampered?

Moreover, Derek and Albert had agreed to meet Unity there and join her Nazi crusade. They told her they weren't diehard Nazis but thought it would be good fun nonetheless. She thought they were good sports and knew they would make for good company, so somehow forgave them their lack of devotion to the cause.

But on her way to the Karlove Vary, Unity was pulled over by the Czech police near the small village of Kamenne Zehrovice, where she was allowed to telephone the British embassy in Prague.

She was extremely annoyed. 'I've been arrested in this small town on my way from Prague to Carlsbad and all my belongings have been seized! They have no right to do this to me. Why have I been arrested?' she gasped into the telephone.

They went through her luggage and soon it wasn't just the cops who were involved, but also the military. She was stripped of some of her documents and they were sent to authorities in Kladno. Not even Senator Wollner had any power to do anything about this.

The police chief took her aside and shook her indignantly.

'Let me go!' she hissed through clenched teeth.

'Listen to me, young lady! We've known all about you since before you stepped into this country, and we've been keeping a close eye on you the whole time here. We consider you a real threat to the Czechoslovak state with your close ties to the Nazi leadership, and it's absolutely disgusting the way you strutted the streets of Prague with a swastika emblem prominently displayed in your lapel; obviously you've been trying to provoke a reaction. Well you got it, missy, you got it!'

'I wasn't asking for any trouble, I was just driving down to the spa! I didn't do anything. You have no right,' she protested.

It wasn't long before the British embassy registered a complaint with the Ministry of Foreign Affairs: 'This British citizen, Miss Unity Mitford, has been subject to unlawful search and seizure. She was stopped 30 kilometers outside of the Czech capital city of Prague for no apparent reason, held against her will for almost 5 hours, and had some of her possessions seized. All this has occurred even though she has not been formally charged with any crime.'

The Czech response put things in perspective: 'Unity Mitford is reportedly well known as an outspoken Nazi and member of Hitler's inner circle. Ignoring all warnings, she drove past a number of roadblocks on her way out of Prague at a time when the country is on high alert and under imminent threat of a Nazi military assault. But you may rest assured that all of her legal possessions shall be returned to her shortly.'

Unity was released and eventually arrived at Karlove Vary, where she met Albert and Derek and told them what had happened.

The next day, when she opened her hotel room door, eager to peruse the spa, there were detectives there. This startled and upset her. She slammed the door in their faces.

She stood behind the door with her ear to it, biting her nails. Were they gone? Did they plan to loiter there all day?

Realising the absurdity of making herself stay inside, she swung the door open again and paid no attention to them whatsoever, going on her merry little way. She would not let anyone, least of all *them*, dictate her behaviour.

She hopped into her car and turned on the ignition. Moments later the detectives came rushing out of the hotel and climbed into another car. She had been expecting just that.

Soon she was racing down the road with the detectives in hot pursuit, tailing her along the city streets. This continued for about a quarter of an hour, until Unity got fed up. She took a sharp turn into a side street and somehow managed to elude them.

In spite of this, Unity got almost all her confiscated belongings back the same day, including a Hitler Youth knife, the swastika flags for her car, and the cherished painting of Hitler. What the authorities refused to return were her swastika badge and her camera and film, which they wanted to develop in case there was anything suspicious there in the way of espionage.

Unity was forced to reluctantly promise that she would leave Czechoslovakia immediately.

Albert and Derek had been detained together with Bobo, but the Czech secret service quickly realised that they had no ties to the Nazis, and both of them were released after a brief questioning. They looked overjoyed to be released, but they found Unity feeling quite blue. It was over the loss of her Nazi badge.

She pouted. 'I'm sorry at its loss, as it is the second one that the Führer has given me. This one was to replace the one that was torn off my dress by the Jews and communists in Hyde Park a few weeks ago. You know, I don't know why, by the way, but most Jews seem to be communist, homosexual and atheist. So that is why I no longer call myself an atheist. At a police post which we were taken to, I was very thoroughly searched. A woman was brought into the police station and took me into a side room, where I had to undress completely, even taking off my stockings, while she minutely examined all my clothes to see if there were any papers hidden in them. I'm surprised she didn't search my cunt.'

Another thing Unity felt depressed about was that her propaganda adventure in Czechoslovakia turned out to be a fiasco, a failure. At least, that was how she saw it. She was terrified that Hitler would be angry with her over it. But on the contrary, he saw it as a touching sign of her loyalty. To her immense joy, she received from him a *third* new swastika button to replace the previous two lost, and the unrecovered camera was also replaced with a new and even better one.

The assault on Unity by 'Jews' in Hyde Park had been thoroughly covered in Julius Streicher's newspaper. For the most part it had not been Jews but anti-fascists in general; however, the stupidly blind and discriminating hate-monger Streicher blamed *everything* bad on the Jews. Now it was the Czechs who were the target of his wrath, and one could read of how in Czechoslovakia she had been 'most revoltingly molested'. 'Is this the kind of reception that an innocent English girl can expect from the barbarous Czechs?' inquired Streicher's *Der Stürmer*. Moreover, if foreigners like Unity trying to move about peacefully in Czechoslovakia were subject to such outrageous treatment, then how much worse were Sudetens being persecuted? Streicher put his propaganda into full swing on this story. The article concluded, 'Luckily, Miss Mitford was with the Sudeten Senator Wollner. With him, she had immunity. There would have been drastic German reprisals if she had been really abused.'

Now back in Munich, feeling she had proven herself to Hitler, Unity decided to take it easy and dedicate herself to recreation – tennis, riding, swimming. She went with her friend Mary to the large stadium with the open-air swimming pool in the Prinzregentenstrasse.

Mary had started going to an international language school to further improve her German and had made friends with various cliques there, even joining the International Student Club. She wanted Unity to meet her new friends, so she took her along.

Unity was statuesquely tall and sexy in her bathing-suit. She could see the heads turning and the eyes roaming over her body. She didn't mind at all. It gave her a fantastic feeling.

Mary introduced Unity to two of her friends, a Peruvian and a Greek. Unity snickered and mercilessly made fun of them to their faces.

She was much nicer to an English boy named Jeff Geoffrey and his Dutch girlfriend, Masha der Porten.

'We love it here in Germany so much, we never want to leave,' said Jeff.

'Oh, I feel the same way!' cried Unity.

She rhapsodised about Nazi Germany and gleefully bragged about her relationship with Hitler, as she did at practically every opportunity. Then she suddenly turned gloomy. She wouldn't let herself be cheered up. She became so miserable, sitting by the edge of the pool and dipping her feet lazily in the water. She whined, 'Hitler didn't invite me to the Obersalzberg. That's where he has his mountainside retreat, the Berghof. It's because of that jealous bitch Eva Braun! She and her bloody crowd are always trying to keep me away from the Führer. Fucking jealousy!'

Disapproving sighs and stares were directed at Unity whenever she wore low-necked dresses or short-skirted dresses or too much lipstick – not to mention her very free and matter-of-fact ways of expressing herself. Hitler's inner circle had other ideas about how the ideal Nazi girl should conduct herself.

One day, Bobo naïvely came up with a long list of people in Britain who she felt would support an alliance with Germany, and an equally long list of those who would need to be shot. She felt there were many who would put on jackboots and dress up and march for him on the streets. That was her way of thinking. She was fanaticism personified.

Unity asked Hitler point-blank: 'Will there be war? I'm so worried and anxious about it. I beg you, promise me there will be no war with Britain. Is there going to be war, please say no!'

'I don't think so,' he replied with a smile. 'I don't want my government buildings bombed.'

'Yes, I knew it! You really do want peace!'

'The question is, does Britain…? You know, I've advised all foreigners to leave, as a precaution. These are unpredictable times…'

'I'm staying,' said Unity in a firm tone.

'What if Britain loses?' said Hitler.

'Even if Germany won, war between Britain and Germany would be the greatest tragedy for you,' said Unity.

'Well, I'm tremendously proud of amassing the greatest army in European history, the greatest army the world has ever seen, but you know my real interests lie in purely peaceful directions. One of my greatest is art and architecture…'

'I'm glad to hear it. You know we're *both* artists.' She smiled.

He smiled back, and then, after a serious pause, he said, 'You know, I think that friendship between England and Germany is still possible. The German people desire it. And if I can bring it about, I would be deified. I would prefer an alliance with your country than with Italy. The Axis with Italy and Japan won't last. But you British are Aryans, just like us. We *should* be allies.'

'If only Mosley's Fascists could win an election and gain control of the British government, war could be easily avoided.'

'No thanks to all the corrupt and deceptive tools of democracy, the British people as a whole haven't embraced fascism,' said Hitler. 'Mosley's blackshirts haven't done the job by legal means. They will need to use dirty violent, unlawful tactics to overthrow the government and gain control by force. Only then, when the British people get used to fascism and see it's the right way, only then will they embrace it. With Nazism it was the same thing when I think back to our party's humble beginnings. We were laughed at and attacked just the same. And look at us now…'

Hitler then lightened the mood by doing some impressions of people. He was good at doing imitations of senior party members like Göring, Goebbels and Himmler, and did an especially good Mussolini. The table erupted with laughter.

His very best imitation, however, he left for last. It was a caricature of himself.

Unity lost herself in hysterics, which brought tears to her eyes. She pressed her wrists down against her crotch, stuttering, 'Th-this is t-too much! I'm going to pee myself!'

Hitler's birthday party. Unity was of course invited. She sat beside him, checking out all the many gifts he had received, a whopping horde of them.

'I hardly know which present to open first,' said Hitler with a laugh.

He grabbed one that appeared to be a painting and tore the wrapping paper. The room gasped an audible sigh as everyone's eyes were seized by a life-sized nude portrait of Hitler in a triumphant pose, sword in his hand raised above his head. 'It was no doubt painted by some admirer!' exclaimed Hitler. 'Wonderful. I love it!'

He and no one else would know that it was an anonymous gift from Unity herself. As uninhibited as she was, she was a little too embarrassed to reveal that it was her work. It wasn't all modesty. She was afraid of what many in the inner circle might think or say.

After the presents, Unity begged him to do his imitations again, and he did a new one of Chamberlain that knocked Unity out of her chair.

For her own birthdays, Hitler would give Bobo a pocketknife, a pistol, the swastika badge, and the camera. He gave her a chain, but never jewels. Unity took this as a hint that he didn't think of her romantically. *Does Eva Braun get jewels?* she wondered. Hitler sometimes sent Bobo flowers or chocolates, but she didn't read too much into that.

Eva Braun cornered her at one point at the party. 'I am mistress to the greatest Nazi in Germany. What a pity for you that Hitler hasn't taken *you* as his mistress.'

Unity felt like pulling Eva by the hair. That was her first impulse. But instead, she replied calmly and coolly, 'There is a great thrill in desiring the unobtainable.'

Unity was next approached by the British ambassador to Germany. 'Heil Hitler!' she bellowed out to him after clicking her heels and giving the Nazi salute, just as he reached out to shake her hand.

He was dumbfounded, but somehow remembered to make his usual retort, which was 'Rule Britannia!'

They laughed at each other. He joked, 'I suppose if I now start singing 'God Save the King', you'll start singing 'Horst-Wessel-Lied' and we'll see which of us can sing louder and drown the other one out.'

Unity was very amused by his sense of humour. He showed a lot of interest in her, following her around and flirting with her all night, but it was not to be. Bobo had come to Hitler's birthday party with Albert, and, when it was over, she left on his arm.

They went outside to smoke a pipe of hashish. She was being introduced to it for the first time by Al. Sitting on an isolated park bench, they were smoking away, enjoying the calm evening air, when Al started making disparaging remarks about the Führer.

Unity shoved him, punched him in the shoulder.

'Ow!' he exclaimed.

'Don't ever say that again!' she spat.

She ran away and disappeared into the shadows of the park forest. Al ran after her apologetically, but she eluded him in the darkness.

After venting for hours, and furious as ever – although in a calmer mood – she finally made her way to her flat. Mary was in but Unity didn't even acknowledge her as she came in still huffing and puffing. She lay down in bed, and picked up *Mein Kampf* to read.

'Could that baby face of yours really look angry?' said Mary, sitting down beside her. 'Are you going to tell me what happened?'

'I never want to see Al again,' said Unity. 'He is the stupidest boy I've ever known.'

Bobo was on her last holiday in England, although she did not realise it. It was approaching the end of 1938 – the beginning of the last peaceful winter before all hell broke loose and the planet was chewed up and swallowed by the crushing jaws of war.

She found herself in the dock at a courtroom in the town of Chatham. She had been charged with speeding. It was just like Unity to enjoy exceeding the speed limit, to break the rules for kicks.

The policeman who had stopped her had asked, 'Do you know how fast you were going?'

'I have just come back from Germany where there is no speed limit, and I'm afraid I forgot the limit after four months' absence,' she argued.

'But in addition to this, you passed a pedestrian crossing without stopping. How do you excuse *that* then?'

'Oh, well, I blew my horn and the pedestrians wisely skirted out of the way,' she giggled.

But the policeman did not.

She was fined ten shillings by the judge.

Unity and Jessica could never agree on politics and loved to debate it whenever Bobo was back from Germany.

Unity said, 'Hitler is a dreamer of those dreams capable of fulfillment; take into account his genius for achieving the impossible. Friendship with Britain is one of those dreams, and more than that, an expression of our solidarity. One of the foundations of Nazi ideology is the racial theory. Germans believe the Aryan race to be the greatest in the world, which indeed it is. The British are an Aryan people as well. Therefore, the interests of our two countries coincide both humanly and politically. The German Army, the Royal Navy and their two air forces combined would police the world and keep peace in our time. Our super-race will live in fascist utopian freedom and superiority. It is predestined by Nature.'

'I more or less agree,' said her mother, 'but I hate the term "Nazism", for I have nothing against the Jews or any other race, be it black, brown, yellow or *green* for all I care! Politics should be without any racial policy. It is non-racial fascism which will create true equality, eliminate class warfare, raise living standards and strengthen religion, unlike its deadly opponent, Bolshevism.'

'Ha! Democracy and fascism are not on the side of the people, of equality or freedom!' exclaimed Jessica. 'You must be joking! Throw your *Mein Kampf* into the trash, Unity, and get a copy of *The Communist Manifesto*! Communism alone is truly government of the people, by the people, and for the people! Lenin's message is the hope of the future! All other systems and ideologies lead only to oppression and inequality! Forget about Hitler's precious dreams for the select few, forget these stupid pseudo-scientific theories about a Nordic super-race that treats all others as inferior. Mother, I'm pleased we agree on this score, but I don't share your other views about fascism.'

'You're so wrong about everything, Jess,' said Unity in a hiss.

Jessica abruptly turned to her and said, 'You really ought to learn how people think, and how they'll think of you.'

'If only you would go to Germany and could talk to Hitler, you would understand.'

'Oh yes, he is the saviour who can do no wrong,' she replied sarcastically, rolling her eyes.

'Yes! And that is how the King of England ought to be.'

'Even if you did whatever you thought necessary, you can never truly be one of them, never be truly accepted as one of them. You're Unity Mitford, the English girl. You don't realise what you owe to England and to your family. Whatever Hitler asks you to do, you'll do it, which shows that your morals have gone.'

Unity threw a tantrum: 'You! You would do anything for that mass-murdering pig, Stalin! He kills his own countrymen, that one!'

When Unity arrived back to Germany in the spring of 1939, she decided that as fond as she was of Mary, it was time to have her own flat in Munich. This was not long after Kristallnacht, the Nazi pogrom during which ninety-one Jews were killed and over 25,000 were deported to death camps. In addition, some 200 synagogues were burned down and thousands of Jewish businesses and homes were smashed and looted.

Hitler arranged for his private office to dispossess the Jewish residents of four apartments and he gave Unity a choice of which one she wanted to move into.

Unity made a visit to each of the four flats in May, eager to scrutinise them to see which one was best for her. She was quite peeved to enter one of them and find the owners still inside.

'What are you doing here? You're to be out by tomorrow,' said Bobo.

The owners were a man and his wife, the wife weeping while her husband tried to comfort her by putting his arms around her. They sat on the living-room sofa and looked up pitifully at Unity, but said nothing.

Coolly and callously, Unity went from room to room, and nodded. 'Yes, this shall be my new home,' she said. She started talking about where each article of her furniture would go in each room, saying mockingly to the resident couple, 'Your old sofa simply will not do... and what dreadfully ugly curtains you've got... I'll need to get those changed immediately.' She went on and on about how improved the place would be after she was moved in.

The wife wept even more bitterly while Unity emotionlessly and matter-of-factly spoke about colour coordination and the decorations she would add to the flat as soon as it was vacant.

Her words and actions were cold-blooded and deliberate. Her Nazi fanaticism had blinded her emotions and numbed her conscience. She was hardly cognizant of the heartless cruelty she was showing these people. To her mind, these Jews were not human beings, but rather animals. No, worse – they were monsters. The Nazi doctrine had dehumanised them. They were now nothing more than a plague on humanity. Therefore, she felt no reason to feel the slightest empathy for them. The real plague, of course, was her own racial hatred. She didn't consider for an instant that she was victimising this man and woman. They were simply an unsightly and annoying barrier between her and her new home, a barrier that would very quickly and easily be removed.

This incident was the perfect example of anti-Semitism, whose logical conclusion was the Holocaust.

Before moving in, Unity called for a pest control inspection of the flat. She wanted to make sure there were no vermin or rats 'because Jews have lived here'. She also added a new paint job and put in a new carpet.

The address of this new home of hers was Agnesstrasse 26, Flat 4, and her telephone number was 372-338. It was in a rather affluent and trendy location, and the apartment complex was rather elegant-looking. Her flat sat on the third and top floor and was quiet and spacious, including three rooms and a large kitchen. A housekeeper would look after the place.

Not only had Hitler had a hand in stealing the flat from its previous owners, he also took it upon himself to furnish it, buying a dining-room table and English-style chairs to accompany it, to Bobo's pleasant surprise. What pleased her most, however, was the new sofa, which replaced the sunken, tattered old one that she had seen on her initial visit.

Expensive, well-crafted new furniture, colourful new decorations, vases full of exquisite flowers strewn about, a newly popular cut-pile carpet, and everything imaginable to make her new abode look modern, chic and beautiful. Just as with her car, she had swastika flags hanging from her bedposts.

'That's too much,' said Mary about the flags when she came to see her best friend.

'That's how I want it,' was Bobo's only answer.

Hitler's portrait hung above her bed, and there was a little bedside table with a signed and framed photograph of Hitler. But Bobo had coloured in the eyes and lips.

'I did that,' she admitted, 'because it looks so nice and I like to kiss him there before I go to bed.'

Unity stepped over to her writing table and slowly, provocatively, opened one of the drawers, staring at Mary the whole time.

'What are you doing?' asked Mary, slightly perplexed. Not that she wasn't used to Unity's weirdness.

Unity abruptly flashed out a revolver, making Mary jolt and sigh aloud. This made Unity giggle as she waved it around in the air. She then pointed it at Mary and pretended to aim.

'Oh Bobo, stop it!' Mary gasped.

Unity turned the gun on herself. 'I might have to kill... myself...'

It was scary, the way she was handling the loaded weapon.

'Put it back in the drawer, won't you?' said Mary.

'As you wish.'

Unity and Mary were no longer room-mates, but still the closest of chums. They went riding and swimming together, as before. Mary's parents weren't happy about it; they wrote her letters saying how dangerous it was in such perilous times to be aligning herself with someone who was so vilified as a Nazi sympathiser in the British press.

But Mary had fun with Unity. She was glad to escape parental meddling in her life. Her mother, especially, had always been suffocatingly authoritarian, telling her what she could or couldn't do, even in her adulthood. 'Behave at all times and avoid wild behaviour' seemed to be her mother's mantra.

What drew her and Unity together? Mary had always been a little in awe of Unity, having been made submissive by her severe and austere upbringing. She looked up to Unity for having the courage to live as she liked. She did everything that she wanted to do. Who wouldn't want to be that free? Unity let no one dictate her lifestyle or behaviour, not even her beloved Führer, whom she worshipped and respected above all else. For example, she wore make-up and lipstick against his express wishes and marked disapproval. It was this freedom in Unity that Mary found irresistible, and they had a lot of fun in each other's company. That was what held them together – not politics, or their English background. Moreover, they both came from the same class and didn't need anything from each other.

Unity and Mary often rode horses, but once they were riding bicycles alongside one another in the park.

Mary told her what her parents were writing. 'Such unbearable letters,' she sighed. 'Mother says, "If your Unity doesn't work and get herself a real interest in life, she is going to commit suicide. She needs to take a job or a husband, otherwise she'll end up taking her life."'

'Your mother's right,' said Unity, gazing at Mary, who looked startled by her remark. 'But she doesn't realise that I have this job, this duty in life. I know I can never be Hitler's bride, but I'm spiritually and emotionally wedded to him and the Nazi party. It's the whole meaning of my life. And it's wonderful… He's wonderful…'

'All right, Hitler may be as wonderful as all that, but what about what he's doing to the Jews?'

Unity pointed her finger at Mary with conviction. 'What he's doing to them is wonderful too,' she answered with a mindless snarl.

Mary was inclined towards fascism, since one couldn't help but be slowly infected by Nazism after years of living in Germany under the Third Reich. It was a contagion that almost everyone around her had caught. The atmosphere of the time and place was by 1939 solidly Nazi. But even so, Mary found Unity's racially prejudiced attitude fundamentally unjust.

Quite out of character for her, and acting purely on the impulse of the moment, Mary responded outright, 'Please don't speak to me about Jews. You talk such arrant nonsense about them.'

'What's got into you? Don't you stand by our beloved Führer?' asked Unity.

'Of course I do,' said Mary. 'But I don't like how he's dealing with the Jewish problem. There must be a more fair, humane and reasonable solution.'

'If that's how you feel about it,' said Unity, 'maybe you should leave Germany.'

Mary warned Unity, 'You know, if it comes to war, we would be far safer and better off in our own country.'

'If there is a war, I shall stay right here… and I'll be on the German side,' said Bobo.

'But how could you? If he wins the war, he'll put millions of people in concentration camps.'

'Millions of people died in the Armenian massacres of 1915 or the Great Purge in Communist Russia in recent years, and millions are dying of hunger in the Ukraine right now and nobody takes any real notice, but as soon as people are put behind bars in Hitler's Germany, the world cries with outrage!'

Mary left Munich for the safer harbour of the countryside and many other British people started leaving Germany altogether, heading back to their native England in anticipation of a possible war. It was no longer safe for foreigners in Germany, especially if the foreigner came from a country at odds with Hitler's Reich.

Unity received telegram after telegram and telephone call after telephone call from friends and family begging her to flee Germany, but these pleadings fell on deaf ears (or blind eyes). Stubborn and resolute rebel that she was, she had no intention of forsaking her Führer. After all, he was her spiritual saviour and political messiah. It would make no sense to leave. When he spoke at rallies, there was so much electricity in the air that she felt she was in the magical presence of Jesus Christ, but a non-Jewish Aryan Christ, which was even better. She even prayed to Hitler every night before going to bed, and claimed that her prayers were always answered.

Rumours were spreading that there would be war.

Almost all of Unity's friends were now away, having left the country or gone into hiding in fear of the coming military conflict. She would sit by herself in the Osteria, with the appearance of one who was weighed down by a huge boulder and wouldn't be able to lift it off and get back up on her feet; her posture looked so sunken in her chair and her mood was so lonely and dejected – like someone suffering from acute melancholia or chronic inertia. Such sadness and distress.

Magda Goebbels waved to her from the restaurant window outside. Unity spotted her and waved back. Magda was with her husband, the Minister of Propaganda. Unity signalled for them to join her, but they walked on.

Eventually, her friend Derek came in through the front entrance like a beaming light of hope, approached her table, and immediately pulled her out of her pit of despair.

'Oh God, you don't know how glad I am to see you!' she said.

Her enthusiasm startled him slightly. 'You must be surprised I'm still here,' he replied with a grin. 'I've decided to weather the storm. I figure it's just as dangerous to be in England anyway, probably more so, since Germany can take England any day of the week. Besides, I think it'll be all over before Christmas. Maybe even in a few weeks. But Al's already fled.'

'Oh, don't talk to me about Al,' she said with a grimace. 'What a traitor.'

Derek gave her a puzzled expression. 'But being English, aren't you torn in two? Where does your loyalty lie?'

Unity didn't answer and instead changed the subject: 'Here, try some of my chicken; the Führer pre-ordered it for me as he said he wouldn't be able to make it here today. Oh yes, the Führer likes to buy me things, whether it's chocolates or chicken.'

Derek patriotically retorted, 'In that case, I'd rather have sausage.'

Hitler signed a mutual non-aggression pact with Stalin.

'So, you see, here is proof I am interested in peace,' said Hitler, lunching with Unity at the Osteria as usual. 'I sign what amounts to a peace treaty with the Red Menace – in the interest of avoiding war. Next I expect the Poles to give in to me as the Austrians and Czechs have done before them. Then Britain must simply bow to my reasonable demands, and if they do, then all will be well. You don't need to worry about anything. Stay in your comfortable new apartment in the Agnesstrasse until the crisis dies down. This so-called conflict will be over shortly without a single shot fired. The only thing Britain needs to do is follow a policy of appeasement and I will not threaten or do any harm to your homeland. There will be peace and friendly cooperation between our nations, for which you have so vigorously campaigned and which is your dearest wish, as it is mine. In a few weeks this will all be settled.'

'Then I'll get to see you more often, won't I?'

'Yes.'

'You'll invite me to the Berghof?' said Unity with puppy-dog eyes, well aware that Eva Braun always went there with him.

'Of course, if you like,' replied Hitler.

'You know what I really hate? I'm never alone with you in your rooms. It's so wonderful to be alone with you and sit at your feet, but then Hesse or Bruckner or somebody has to walk in and sit with us. And even when you ask them to leave, they soon waltz back in. It's horrid!'

Eva Braun had a way of ensuring that there was no possibility of any real intimacy between this star-struck English girl and her man. Unity learned from a reliable maid that Hitler and Eva Braun shared a bed at the rural getaway, the Berghof, where she, Unity, had never been invited. She no longer had the luxury of being in denial about the fact that Eva Braun was his mistress. Unity was as jealous as can be. She felt no jealousy towards other women in Hitler's company, for example Sigi Laffert, because she knew Sigi was in love with a fellow named Hansi, not Hitler. *But that Eva! How dare she? If I can't have him, no other woman should be able to!* thought Unity. *And what was all that talk he fed me about his only mistress being Germany – and that he had no sex drive?*

Unity felt rejected, disappointed, misled… but of course not nearly enough to turn against her Führer. By that stage, she was utterly and fanatically sold on him.

At their next meeting, Hitler stunned Unity with the news: 'I now doubt the possibility of a peaceful settlement with Britain.'

Hitler had been hoping that after threatening to crush Poland quickly and decisively, Britain would be very eager to sign for peace with Germany, but he was mistaken. Britain rejected Hitler's offer. Hitler was deeply offended by the slight. He would need to teach the British a lesson. There would be war.

Unity had thought that she would play the part of the heroine and a world war would be averted, like in a simple fairytale. Reality was different.

The British ambassador to Germany bumped into Unity on the street by chance. It was near the end of August 1939. 'I'm surprised to still see you here,' he told her quite earnestly. 'We may be on the outbreak of war.'

She shrugged her shoulders. 'Well, when you warn British subjects to leave, don't warn me, because I intend to stay.'

He told her a story about Nazis transporting a group of Jews to some island on the River Danube and leaving them there for dead.

She replied, 'That's the way to treat them. I wish we could do that in England to our Jews. Leave them stranded on a reef somewhere far, far offshore and then wait for the tide to come in.'

'Oh, come now. Have you no heart? You don't really mean that.'

'Oh, I do. With all my heart.'

Having met the ambassador, Unity decided she would have a face-to-face with the consul as well.

She entered the consulate and gave everyone her typical 'Heil Hitler' salute, including the British consul himself. But he hardly acknowledged her gesture, and said nothing. He didn't even rise from his seat. He appeared troubled, moody.

'How's the situation?' she asked.

'Very serious,' he replied sharply. 'All the British are leaving tomorrow and I advise you to go too.'

'I don't contemplate it for a minute,' she told him.

'Then you no longer have the protection of Great Britain.'

'I have the much better protection of the Führer,' she retorted with a wink.

'You're as silly as the man who told me he wouldn't be leaving because he had tickets for a Wagner concert next week.'

'Oh, who's he? I must get to know him! Sounds like my kind of fellow.'

Unity made a point of visiting Hitler that evening. 'Is there really going to be a war?' she asked.

'Ah, that all depends on your Mr Chamberlain,' Hitler replied.

'If there is, I'll shoot myself. I can't bear the thought of the land of my birth and the land of my ideal destroying each other as enemies; my beloved homeland and the new home I've grown to love, Germany, tearing each other to bits. With every fibre of my being, I long to see Britain and the German nation closely united. I am convinced, I know for a fact, that together we can achieve a world dominion. We should be allies!'

'My dear Bobo, you know I agree. I strongly agree. Britain is an Aryan nation. We're all Anglo-Saxons. I believe that is the term you use. I wish we could unite as allies against the Red Menace in the east. I will give them a chance. But if your government will not see reason, Britain must be conquered. And I will put your Mosley in charge. I have plans for Mosley in Britain just as I already have plans for Heydrich in Czechoslovakia.'

'The British are thorough cowards, but there comes a point when they will fight,' said Unity. 'We must not have another war like the Great War of 1914.'

'What do you know about it?' said Hitler condescendingly. 'You were barely born. I was fighting in the trenches, wondering if each new day would be my last.'

'Say what you will, Wolf,' she said, for the first time daring to address him so intimately. 'If you come to an accommodation with

Britain and America, your victory is assured and you will be Emperor of Europe. And your Third Reich will truly last a thousand years.'

Unity became obsessed with sitting on her carpet in front of the radio in her flat, listening intently to the news. Her attention was hooked by every report and newsflash. These wireless broadcasts would guide her destiny and decide her fate, she knew. To live or to die. That was the question. That was what was at stake. Her ears remained glued to the radio at all times, except when she had to go out to eat. But she was sure to come straight back as soon as possible so as not to miss another update.

Then came what she and everybody had been dreading. Bad news. Poland refused to capitulate to Hitler's demands. War was indeed inevitable.

It was 1 September. Munich was enjoying clear blue sunny skies. Unity wanted to take advantage of the fine weather, so she put on her swimsuit and started tanning on her balcony, bathed in soothing sunshine.

Letters arrived from the mailman. Letters from Diana and Jessica. Unity checked her mail slot and wrote quick replies.

As Bobo was getting dressed to go out that evening for another lonely dinner, the German military was invading Poland.

Unity found the streets of Munich pitch-black. The whole city was under curfew. A compulsory blackout.

The British gave Hitler their non-negotiable ultimatum: begin immediate withdrawal from Poland, or face the consequences. The Führer ignored the message. The Second World War was beginning.

Mary telephoned Unity late that night. 'I can't sleep, can you?' she said. 'What do you think is going to happen? I'm afraid.'

Unity's aim had been to convince Hitler to shy away from another war, especially one between Britain and Germany. She had made it clear to him in no uncertain way that if she could not prevent a war between her native land and the land she had grown to love, the price for her failure would be suicide.

Bobo had shown off her pistol to Mary on the day that she was given it as a gift from the Führer. She had no permit, but she loved to take it out for target practice anyway. She knew that Mary knew of her intent to use it on herself if circumstances drove her to it.

'I don't know. What are *you* going to do?' Unity paused. 'I don't want to live if—'

Mary cut her off: 'I'm out of town right now, but I'll be back in Munich by Monday morning, so don't do anything foolish until then, and we'll see each other and talk about what we'll do for the best of both of us, all right? There's no good reason at all to shoot yourself. Are you listening? Bobo, I beg you to wait until we can meet and decide what's next.'

'What's to decide?' said Unity in a weak and gloomy voice.

'Well, for one thing, we're supposed to go riding together, remember? Everyone says this war won't last very long at all, so make no hasty moves.'

But Unity's mind was elsewhere. Unreachable. She dropped the telephone onto its hook.

Mary tried calling back, but Unity refused to pick up.

Unity slept until noon. It had not been a sleepful night. She threw the bedcovers aside and slowly inched towards her writing table, just as slowly opening the drawer. She took the revolver into her hand and stared at it for what must have seemed an aeon. A tear trickled out of the edge of her eye and her hand started to tremble a little, so she set the weapon down.

She filled a large envelope package with her swastika badge, photographs of Hitler, her autographed copy of his book, and all the other treasured gifts the Führer had ever bestowed upon her. The only things she left out were the portrait and the camera, because they wouldn't fit.

After a quick breakfast, she sped off in her car and stopped at the post office to drop off the letters she had written to Diana and Mary.

She then stopped off at the British embassy and handed the surprised ambassador her package.

'I would like to give you this,' she said in a hasty and breathless tone.

The ambassador momentarily glanced at the big, thick envelope and asked, 'What is it?'

She looked away and started walking, evading the question entirely.

The ambassador called out to her as she hurried down the hall, 'Have no fear, just stay in Munich and keep a low profile, live quietly, keep yourself inconspicuous – nothing foolish, you hear? And I'll see that you come to no harm. I'll be responsible for your safety and make sure nothing happens to you.'

Unity didn't react to anything he said, just rushed down the staircase and away almost as fast as her stride could carry her.

The sealed packet she had forced into the ambassador's hands didn't seem to stir his curiosity. After all, war had been declared and he was extremely busy with other correspondence. Finally, when he got around to her package and emptied its contents onto his desk, he found a letter of farewell – a dramatic goodbye addressed directly both to her Führer and, indirectly, to her very own life as well. 'Be merciful to my country,' she wrote Hitler. Along with the letter, there were of course her beloved souvenirs, including her precious party badge made of gold.

The ambassador leaped from his chair and tried to alert others. This was a tragedy he would have to avert. But where was Unity? She had disappeared in her car. She loved to be behind the wheel, so free… and she always drove too fast.

Professor Honigschmitt veered lazily into the Englischer Garten in Munich. It was so peaceful and quiet, warm but not too hot, a fine early September day.

Before he had strolled inside more than a hundred paces, a small explosion nearby broke through the air and a young woman slid off her bench, face down.

He ran over to her and turned her onto her back. 'Oh my Lord! Are you all right, young lady?' he cried, slightly panicky.

Unity's fluttering eyelids opened somewhat. 'Oh professor,' she feebly moaned, recognising him as her mathematics teacher. Almost immediately, she went limp, unconscious. Dead?

There was blood leaking from the side of her head. She had shot herself in the right temple.

The professor stood up and started shouting for help.

Within moments, a growing crowd converged on the scene.

The ambassador back at the embassy had already notified the police, and an ambulance was summoned by the professor within a quarter of an hour.

Some people swarming around her body thought she might be dead and that the only thing she had to look forward to was a post-mortem, but then her head moved slightly and she slowly moved a shaky hand up to touch her wound.

She was raced to the emergency clinic.

No one knew who she was. She didn't have her purse or any kind of ID. Her appearance indicated that she was upper-class, but it wasn't until sometime later that she was identified as Unity Mitford, the twenty-five-year-old daughter of an English aristocrat.

'It looks pretty hopeless,' said the head surgeon after examining the injury. 'The bullet is embedded in a deep and dangerous area of the brain that controls mobility. Operation is of course always possible, but in this case, very risky. If we leave it alone, she's almost guaranteed another ten years of life. If we operate now, we have a 50 per cent chance of success, but it could also end badly, with paralysis, brain damage or even death. With no immediate threat to her life, I suggest we side with caution and not operate at this time…'

A personally shocked and distraught Hitler, when he heard the terrible news, paid all expenses for a large private room in the hospital, with personal nurses to look after Unity at all hours.

THE AFTERMATH

Mary checked her mail the next Monday morning and almost fainted when she read Unity's letter. It was like a last will and testament. It included the chilling lines:

Here are the keys to my flat. I'm killing myself. You know why. When you get this, I will already be gone. Please contact my family with regard to my belongings.

Mary went to Unity's flat with the key, but the lock to her front door had already been sealed over with tape by the police so that no one could enter.

Lord and Lady Redesdale were informed of their daughter's close brush with death, and they sought permission to see her right away. But with bureaucracy everything takes time; it proved no easy task.

After several days, Unity regained consciousness, but her ability to write and speak was impaired, and she couldn't wash or change or feed herself without assistance. She looked as pale as a corpse. Her eyes would open, but her mind wasn't completely 'there' yet. Sometimes it was difficult to ascertain her needs or wishes. She would garble her words: 'Can you give me that table on the fruit?' Whenever she tried to walk, she was overcome with vertigo.

An X-ray was taken, revealing that the bullet was stuck in the back of the skull. The wound gave her face a puffy appearance. The doctors made regular check-ups on her condition.

It took about a week before Unity started recognising people she knew. A little while after that, she could walk on her own without help.

Mary visited her as soon as she could. Unity could see in her eyes how dismayed she was by the sad transformation of her best friend.

'Do you regret what you've done?' Mary asked.

But Unity side-tracked the issue by responding, 'That was a terrible fall I had... that's why I'm ill.'

She knew very well what she had done to herself, but she didn't want to upset herself by talking about it and preferred to give the impression of not knowing what had happened.

Magda made regular hospital visits, prompted by Hitler, who said, 'Help our Unity find her way back to the land of the living.'

Unity's blank stares soon turned to normal eye-contact with those who tried to engage with her, and normal conversation returned to her lips.

Her package of cherished Nazi keepsakes was returned to her. Magda took it to her as she lay in bed, and when Unity saw it, she swiftly yanked the envelope away from her and buried it under her covers, as if to hide not only the package itself but also her embarrassment over the tragic incident.

Mary got a late-night telephone call from one of Unity's personal nurses, who sounded concerned because the swastika broach was inexplicably gone.

'She denies it, but I think she's swallowed it!' said the nurse.

'My God!' gasped Mary. 'Does she not want to recover?'

Unity had indeed tried to choke herself to death, had failed. The doctors used a probe in her stomach and retrieved the swastika broach. Again, she refused to say anything about it.

Hitler had been tied down by the invasion of Poland, but he finally found the time to see Unity at the clinic. He was led into her sickroom.

'My Führer!' exclaimed Unity instantly.

They had a warm heart-to-heart talk, and then outside her room Hitler talked with the doctors about her recovery.

'Will you be extracting the bullet?' he inquired.

'We considered it, but rejected the idea. It's not necessary,' they explained.

'Yes, I see. You don't want the responsibility of a famous corpse on your scalpel,' Hitler retorted.

It was a 6.35 Walther that Unity had shot herself with, like a Baby Browning. She had always kept it in her purse. Shooting was just one of the activities that she and Mary had enjoyed together, along with skiing, swimming and riding. They had both learned how to use pistols at the local firing range.

'Why did Hitler give you the gun?' said Mary. 'What a strange gift. Why give you that?'

'For self-defence, of course,' said Unity.

'Or did he just want you to do away with yourself?'

'Oh hah-hah! Very funny.'

'It's not as ridiculous as it may sound,' suggested Mary. 'Isn't that what he did with his precious niece Geli many years earlier – give her a gun as a gift? Except in that case, the suicide attempt was successful.'

Everything that Unity had hoped for, everything that she had lived for, had come crumbling down. She was firmly convinced that there would never be peace, and that Hitler would never be her husband. That self-inflicted shot to the head was the self-imposed punishment for her failure to meet those crucial goals, and the end result was a disastrous bang that had not only shattered her brain, but also symbolised the death of all of her dreams. It was all beyond repair now.

Unity had written Hitler a goodbye letter before the attempt to end her life. It was a very passionate note. She wrote:

I love you more than anything – yes, I am in love with you. But your heart is elsewhere. Eva Braun has made you hers. And you refuse to make friends with my England. That is why I must die.

Hitler had been preoccupied and focused on the war, but the news about Unity had upset him deeply. He cared deeply for her, of course. But he also saw it as a bad omen.

'And what will be done with her dog, Rebel?' he asked, like the dog lover that he was.

It had been thanks to Hitler that Unity had received the best medical treatment available. He had always felt that their destinies were woven together, and he wanted her to be well.

Everyone in his inner circle who had been against Unity got together and approached Hitler. They expressed their regret and apologised for their wrongful suspicions. Hitler broke down in tears in front of them and sobbed. 'You see, she was nothing but an idealist, not a spy. She was what she seemed to be all along. But she couldn't have stopped the war.'

Hitler had flowers sent to her. He did feel for her. The British ambassador and the Goebbelses expressed similar sympathy.

Magda came fairly often, but Mary visited Unity the most. They spoke together about Bobo.

'She wasn't a happy person, not at all,' said Magda.

'As I understand it,' said Mary, 'she was always a kind of outsider in her family, never quite good enough compared to her more accomplished sisters. In fact, she was an outsider with virtually everybody, really. She was very cold. She had never known any love. I'm not a bit surprised that she shot herself, poor dear girl.'

It was arranged that Unity would be transferred to Switzerland, where an English doctor would be awaiting her, and from there back to England.

A special railway carriage was summoned and made ready for Unity. It was large, private and comfortable, equipped for transporting injured or wounded persons. Unity left in the company of a personal nurse.

The train crossed over into Switzerland through Bregenz and the English doctor received her in Berne with raised eyebrows. 'What's all this talk about her not speaking?' he asked. 'She has been singing Hitler's praises.'

'I was mute because they would not let me take roses *from Hitler* back to England with me,' said Unity with a pout.

Mary could have joined Unity on the journey home, but decided she would rather stay in Germany. She had fetched Unity's clothes to her in the hospital, and packed up and cleaned out her Agnesstrasse apartment with the help of the cleaning lady who had been housekeeping it. Unity's personal items were also sent to England, with the exception of anything Nazi (some of which was kept and most of which was destroyed by Mary, so that it wouldn't cause her friend trouble with English customs and other authorities).

Unity took the cross-channel ferry from Calais to Folkstone, and as soon as the ship was tied to port, the chief of police and the chief immigration officer both boarded and entered Unity's cabin. They questioned Unity, checked her passport, and went through various documents.

When they had finished with the search, Unity was lifted out of bed with her blanket folded around her, and put on a stretcher.

Her father ran up to her as she was taken off of the ship and kissed her face multiple times.

She was accosted by journalists as she was being shuffled into the ambulance. They repeatedly asked what had happened to her, but she just mumbled that she didn't know, couldn't remember, adding: 'But I'm glad to be in England... even if I'm not on your side.'

She didn't stay in Folkstone for long, and as soon as she had some breakfast in her belly, the ambulance headed off again, this time to the Radcliffe Infirmary in Oxford.

She was examined by one of the best neurosurgeons in the country, who concluded, 'Her general health is good and the wound from which she suffered and for which she was skilfully treated has healed in a normal and satisfactory manner. After consultation, it has been decided that no operation is advisable or desirable.'

Unity was put in Ward 1. It had six private patient rooms, one of which was taken up by her.

The newspapers were able to milk the story for all it was worth, with photographs of Unity on the stretcher. 'I have been offered £5,000 for her story,' said her father. 'I would not even take £25,000. I would not like to make money that way.' He drifted in and out of the infirmary. Every day he came to check up on his dear sweet Unity.

Although it was commonly known that Unity had been in Hitler's inner circle for several years, she was not arrested or interrogated upon her return to English soil, partly due to her apparently disabled condition and partly due to her father's political connections. But some of the press and public called for her to be interned. It was debated in the House of Commons, but she was let off the hook by the Home Secretary and it began to look like 'Hitler's British girl' was going to spend the rest of the war as a free woman.

In Britain, many papers said Unity belonged behind bars. The *Daily Mirror* contemplated why 'the Mitford girl, who has been openly consorting with the King's enemies, should go scot free'.

But interrogating her would have been pointless. Her memory was fuddled by the bullet that was still in her brain. 'It's a mercy, I suppose,' said Jessica.

All that Unity could remember was that Hitler once told her that she had nice legs.

'I'm glad to be home,' she said to her sisters. 'I thought you all hated me, but I don't remember why.'

Lady Redesdale wanted to move Unity to a secluded island the family owned called Inch Kenneth, 'where she will be kept safe and out of trouble'. They had sold Swinbrook and bought the little island two years earlier. But Lord Redesdale couldn't live year-round in such an isolated spot and didn't want to be separated from his daughter, so in the end Unity was taken to the family's country cottage in High Wycombe instead.

Mary changed her mind, seized by pangs of conscience, deciding she wanted to be with Unity in her time of trial. Besides, she was lonely without her. She found a way to break the red tape and get back to England, regardless of the risk or danger.

Appearing at the cottage one rainy afternoon, she was met by Unity's father, who said, 'I shall never be able to hold my head up again.'

Mary smiled. 'I would hold my head up higher. It would have been terrible if she had shot herself dead. Now she'll at least have time to repent.'

'Mary, you've been such a true friend to her,' he said after an emotional gulp and a deep pause.

Mary was invited to live at High Wycombe to watch over Unity, as a kind of paid companion and babysitter. It could be quite a task sometimes. Unity would occasionally show a bad temper, or act childishly and do foolish things.

'What time are you going to have your lunch? I think I'll have mine too,' said Unity. And then she said, 'But I'm going out!' Almost in the same breath she added, 'No, I've changed my mind, I'll stay in and we'll have our lunch together.' But then she quickly changed her mind a *third* time and ended up getting ready to go out anyway. 'Oh damn,' she said, checking her purse and running over to Mary, stomping her foot down in irritation. 'I've not got enough change. I gave five shillings to the taxi for a tip last time.'

'Whatever did you do that for?' asked Mary, frowning. 'I'm not going to help you if you're going giving away your money.'

Unity would get up to all sorts of trouble. Sometimes it seemed as if she was left with the mental age of a twelve-year-old. She was unpredictable, fractious, clumsy and incontinent at night (she had to wear nappies as she couldn't control her bladder). At other times she seemed more or less OK.

She liked to lay in the bathtub for long periods of time – up to her neck in the water, motionless, with a scary blank stare in her eyes.

Mary walked in on her once after she had been in the tub for a particularly long time. She was clearly worried about her, and bent down to lift her out of the water.

'What a fright you're giving me!' said Mary. 'Now no more games with me.'

In spite of the best care, Unity was not really herself after the trauma of the gunshot wound.

Diana was still living with Oswald Mosley, and would forever be considered the black sheep of the family for divorcing her husband and becoming Mosley's mistress.

Unity wrote Diana a pathetic little letter. 'I have such a sweet little new puppy, I love my little puppy, love and kisses…' Diana must have been appalled and dismayed by the degree of mental deterioration. She didn't visit Unity or even reply to the letter.

Unity showed little regard for her appearance and started gaining a lot of weight. Even her feet seemed to get bigger, and she would steal her brother Tom's shoes.

That Easter, Jessica remarked, 'You used to be much slimmer.'

But in time she improved a lot – mentally, at least. She displayed a growing capacity to speak sensibly and intelligently about all kinds of things. Strangely and amazingly, Hitler and the Nazi ideology were not to be found on her lips, even though not long before she had talked about little else. Unfortunately, her Führer had proved to be a great and disillusioning disappointment to her in the end, first by rejecting her love, and then by failing to secure a friendly understanding and unified alliance between their two nations.

Rumors spread that her father was a fascist or Nazi sympathiser simply because Unity was his daughter and he had come to fetch her home and offer her refuge and protection. Little did they realise that it was nothing more than paternal love at play. Lord Redesdale adored his Unity. He always had and always would.

But the false allegations wounded him deeply. 'So now I'm a Nazi because I care for the welfare of my daughter as any father should? Rubbish! I have another daughter who is a communist. Does that make me a *Red* also? I resent the undercurrent of suspicion created by all this publicity of money-hungry newspaper publishers eager to sell sensationalistic trash! I find it wounding that I am constantly described as a fascist. I am not, never have been, and am not likely to become a fascist.'

Jessica now saw Unity regularly. Bobo developed a fetish for gloves, so, to make her happy, Jessica bought her expensive fur gloves. Despite their political differences, they were fast friends once again, as in childhood.

Tom died fighting for the British in Burma. They received the news by mail. It was not unexpected, but it came as a shock to the family.

Unity had never been very close with her brother, who seemed unsympathetic to her. She felt much less distressed about the news of his death and more relieved about the fact that he wasn't killed in Germany – meaning that he didn't fight against the Germans but against the Japanese.

In time, in spite of her disillusionment, she tried to re-establish contact with Hitler. But Hitler seemed to have forgotten all about her. 'I love the child,' he said, 'but I cannot speak to her; I know what she would say to me and it would weaken my resolve.' He didn't take her telephone calls; didn't even reply to her letters.

Besides, he had much more important matters on his mind.

Unity was crushed; she felt abandoned by him, by the cause – betrayed. *Is this my reward for so many years of deep friendship and unwavering loyalty?* She now realised that Hitler was never truly interested in an alliance with Britain, but ultimately in world domination. He had lied, lied for all those years, and to her it was the most terrible lie. She recalled things he had said, things she heard him say but hadn't really processed at the time. Now, somehow, these statements he had made flashed crystal-clear in her memory and their deeper meaning sunk in. Even his friendly treaties with Russia, Italy, and Japan were a joke in his mind. He planned to betray, destroy and conquer his own allies *as well*. She remembered that he had once told her this in confidence. And if he was willing to betray an allied country, she realised he was also capable of betraying a personal ally, in this case herself. What mistake had she made, to follow such a phoney, such a liar, such a traitor? Had she betrayed her own country? She started to feel guilty. She started going down to Whitechapel to scrub floors and hand out food to the needy as a sort of self-imposed penance.

'Why didn't you stop me?' she would say about her former love for Hitler and irrational hatred of Jews.

'We tried to,' they would say.

Yet from time to time there were brief moments when she couldn't help but be torn between both sides, unable to completely crush those fading remnants of loyalty towards Hitler. It was too painful for her not to deny his wrongs, since she had believed he had always had the best intentions. Moreover, if she were to admit he was a madman and a monster, what would that say about her? After the war, when the horrible and heartbreaking concentration camp films were shown to the world and everyone saw for the first time the sheer horror of Hitler's Holocaust, Unity would insist, 'That must all be propaganda. There was a typhoid epidemic or something and it's the way of getting rid of the bodies.'

But Hitler was on the way out. She switched her obsession with the Führer for an obsession with religion. Her former atheism was traded for faith. She resolved she would atone for her sins and mistakes and make herself right with God and mankind.

Bobo took to attending the local parish church and volunteering in its charity endeavours. She remembered the vicar, the Revd Float, from childhood – he had been kind and given her words of support when she was a little girl. Now he helped and guided her as an adult as well.

The summer of 1940. Half a year had passed since Unity had arrived home. Hitler's air force was now dropping bombs on her homeland, paving the way for an invasion by sea.

It was a warm, slightly breezy day with beautiful clear skies, and Unity was with her father and Jessica, enjoying a peaceful picnic in the park. Suddenly, the sirens started blaring and people scrambled for the bomb shelters.

Jessica was irate. 'If your Hitler hadn't started the war, we could have stayed to enjoy perfect weather,' she said. 'Now I have my calm and pleasant afternoon ruined by this crap!'

'You will apologise to me for this slander against Hitler or else I will not speak to you again!' Unity shrieked.

'I won't apologise for speaking the truth!' retorted Jessica. 'What's more, if you're a supporter of his, like the Duke of Windsor, then you're just as bad as him!'

'How dare you show such national disloyalty!' said Unity. 'It is our duty as British subjects to support the King whatever he did. The new king is a pitiful and boring, stuttering weakling and his queen is only a common shop girl.'

'Now, now, girls,' said their father, 'let's stop this arguing.' And he ushered them away to safety until the sirens had stopped and the coast was clear.

A day later, Unity told Jessica that she was sorry and that Jessica's comments about Hitler were justified. 'It is I who owe *you* an apology, not the other way around,' Bobo murmured. Immediately, all was well between them.

But the fact that Unity was so often seen out and about meant tongues wagged quite freely about her. Press reporters and photographers stalked and hounded her, persecuting her in print. Even Parliament added its voice to the criticism, discussing the fact that she had been an agitator for the enemy and debating whether or not she should be interned as a pro-Nazi traitor.

Once more, the Home Secretary intervened in her favour: 'My information as to the condition of this person's health and the circumstances in which she is lying does not indicate that there is at present any ground which makes it necessary in the interests of national security to exercise control over her.'

So Unity remained free, but felt alone. She could count on Jessica's friendship of course, but, due to her Nazi past, there were precious few other people outside of the family who treated her as a friend. She was often lonely. Thankfully, books had always been her comfort.

She walked into a bookshop on Curzon Street in the exclusive Mayfair district of London to pick out some new reading material.

Bobo went up to the girl working at the front counter. 'Do you have *Lady Chatterley's Lover* by D. H. Lawrence?' she inquired.

'No, that book is banned,' the shopkeeper replied.

'That's why I want it,' said Unity.

They started chatting and soon seemed quite taken with each other. They spoke casually about everything from current bestsellers to the war situation, when out of the blue Unity said, 'Do you think it is wicked to commit suicide?'

'Uh, I don't think I've ever thought about it,' the shopkeeper said.

This was a common characteristic of Unity's. She would act normal for a prolonged space of time, and then all of a sudden she would do or say something odd or unexpected.

A great regret in her life was that she had wasted all her love and energy on Hitler, a man who would never return her love. She had missed out on finding a husband and having a family. Now it seemed too late.

'All I want from life is a husband, which everyone of course tells me is out of the question. But when I get married, I should like to have ten children. I want at least five – no, six – sons. The eldest will be called Adolf, and all the rest John.'

She browsed the *Matrimonial Times*, shrieking with laughter. 'If no man wants me, I'll become a nurse,' she said. 'The sisters were so good to me in the hospital. In addition, I want to also be a missionary worker in foreign lands. That way I can heal not only their bodies as a nurse but also their souls as a missionary.'

Nazism had poisoned her mind and her blind faith in her false god Hitler had left her disenchanted. He had let her down tremendously. In Hitler's place was left a void, and this void was filled by spiritual faith in God, and a desire – or downright need – to make amends for her former life and to make a positive change.

But Unity was cynical, or rather, realistic, about the war. 'It makes no difference who wins,' she said. 'No side will stand victorious when the human toll is counted.'

Unity became a member of the congregation at All Saints' church, and, as a new member, she was warmly welcomed, which really lifted her spirits and filled her heart and soul with a rich and stimulating sense of gladness. It put a sense of real meaning into her life. Nazism had not been her true calling; *this* was her true calling. That's not to say that she had suddenly become a saint; she still possessed many faults and continued to say and do some bad and silly things, but at least she was on the right path. Her character was improving.

She had to go through a ceremony in the church where she had to stand and shake everybody's hand. 'It's wonderful to have 200 people shaking one's hand,' she said to the Revd Float with a broad smile, 'because *nobody* does that to me now. I'm the most hated woman in England.' That last sentence out of her mouth shrunk her smile a bit, but the continuous parade of handshakes soon restored her good mood.

Her rather unfortunate gift for *faux pas* remained, however. There was a party that evening and Bobo was seated next to Pierre Roy, a sort of political advisor to General de Gaulle. His opening words to her were, 'I expect you speak far better French than I do English.'

She lashed back, 'Thank the Lord, not a word of the beastly language,' without realising in the slightest how offensive her reply would be to him. Then, to make things much worse, she spewed hatred for the French. They had been 'whipped' by the Germans yet again, she said, and had to rely on British and American allies to come to their rescue. They hadn't won a war in 200 years, since Napoleon. It was incredible how everybody kept their composure and let her rant on and on.

After such unpleasantries, Roy tried to change the subject. He didn't dare talk to her about the French Resistance, and instead started talking about the current situation and how the USA would need to join the fight to defeat Hitler.

'The war makes little difference to me,' she said aloud. 'I want to die anyway.'

It was of course chilling for those present to hear her speak this way when they knew of her previous suicide attempt.

Later on that same evening, when everyone was dancing and having fun, Bobo was sitting alone at the table. Charles Ritchie, a young Canadian diplomat, came up to her and sat down beside her.

'Hello, you must be Unity,' he said.

'I hit my left breast over a lamp-post as I was bicycling here,' she blurted. 'Still hurts a little. Not really in the best of moods for dancing.'

'I heard about how you tried to kill yourself. I read about it too. It was in all the papers for a good week or so. I felt so sorry for you.'

'I tried to commit suicide when I was in Germany but now I am a Christian. Not that I believed a word of it, but those people have brought purpose to my life and saved my soul, so I think I owe it to them to be one and believe.'

There was a pause, as Charles searched his mind for something to say. He was intrigued by her and wanted to keep the conversation going.

'I hate the Czechs,' said Unity abruptly in a loud emphatic voice. Then, in a normal tone, she added, 'But that is natural – they tried to arrest me and I had not done anything. I didn't even have the Führer's picture on me as they said I had.' She was either lying, or had forgotten the truth.

'You know what people are thinking and saying about you, I'm sure,' said Charles. 'Your role as Hitler's close English friend does not make you very endearing. But I must say, I like you better than anyone else at this party. You've never been afraid to just be yourself and to hell with what anyone says or thinks. Most of us are cowards.'

But Unity was terribly lonesome and depressed to be excluded by so many people in English society.

'Poor old Bobo,' Unity's mother said, appearing with a cocktail and interrupting their conversation. 'Do be nice to her. She runs up to everybody like a big, wet, shaggy dog, wagging her tail, craving attention, and nobody is nice to her.'

1941.

Unity had a fairly good recovery, but still had rare moments where it was obvious she wasn't completely OK. She would have an occasional dizzy spell and had a slight limp when she walked. Also, certain muscular abilities needed to be regained – in order to write, for example.

Bobo rode her bike around, singing out loud. Most people ignored her. In the congregation she was tolerated, but not truly accepted, just as she had never been truly accepted among the Nazis. The Revd Float, however, sometimes invited her to afternoon tea.

Once, while she was riding her bicycle around the village, she spotted the Revd Float in the churchyard and pedalled up to him.

Casually, she blurted, 'Soon I'll be dead, so I wish to be buried as near as possible to the church, so I can hear the hymn-singing. My favourite hymn is "Praise my Soul, the King of Heaven".'

There was a Miss Jones who ran a canteen for British soldiers. Unity came and helped out a bit, but some people in the village disapproved and put an end to it.

Unity took a fancy to Miss Jones and her sister. People would say, 'You can't have *her* in your house.'

But it was just wartime pettiness and Miss Jones would defend Unity by answering, 'If I'd been close with someone as famous as Hitler, I'd have been flattered too!'

From her own mother, Unity could expect no such defence. Lady Redesdale was finding it hard to come to terms with Tom's death. In her grief, she was all prickles and stings. And Unity became the target of every sting.

'He perished a patriot, fighting for the right cause,' said Lady Redesdale, weeping. 'Unlike you, who are alive and a traitor to your own country...'

Unity exhaled in dismay. 'I adored Hitler at one time, but I was not a traitor.'

Unity finally moved to the small island of Inch Kenneth near Mull off the west coast of Scotland in late July, 1942. With the war still raging and the ever-present controversy surrounding Unity, the Mitford family agreed that it was better to put Bobo away somewhere where people wouldn't know about her anymore, where she could be shielded from the sneers and ridicule of the locals. Inch Kenneth was the perfect spot, a picturesque and secluded little isle far from the prying eyes of the public. There she would finally be left alone.

On the boat crossing, Bobo hit it off with a small boy, and they ran around the deck, goofing around, pretending to shoot each other like cops and robbers.

'I had a real revolver and I used to shoot stuff with it,' she said to him.

'Like what?' he asked.

'Oh, like myself for instance!' she said with morbid wit.

He laughed unbelievingly. 'Why are you going to Inch Kenneth?'

'I haven't been well. I'm going to stay with my dad. He says I don't get enough good food.'

'Is he a good cook?' he asked stupidly.

'Oh no,' said Unity with a laugh.

'Is he a good daddy?'

'Certainly. What an extraordinary question,' Unity sighed.

Inch Kenneth was about half a mile offshore and Unity was much taken with the island as soon as she beheld it in the nearby distance – the rugged hilly landscape, its grass emerald-green. About 150 acres altogether. Standing tall amid this was a big, white, roomy mansion that Unity and her father would make their new home. Lord Redesdale had decided he would dedicate himself to her care. Beside the mansion, beyond a sheep-grazing pasture, were the ancient and decrepit stone remains of an unroofed and abandoned chapel, where Unity would improvise religious services. Father and daughter would be closeted together in seclusion, locked away from the real world, as if nothing had changed and Europe was not being ruined by another world war.

Down the road lived a family who helped run the property, the Campbells. They had many children and Unity enjoyed visiting them. When she saw Mrs Campbell's newborn in the cradle, Bobo asked, almost begged, if she could hold her, yapping on and on about how much she wished she could have children of her own. She even made a pink pram-cover for the baby, and brought stuffed toy rabbits for the others.

One Sunday morning, a stranger intruded on their worship at the chapel ruins. Lord Redesdale whispered to Unity to look over her shoulder, and there stood a man in a belted overcoat, with a lock of hair plastered down on his forehead, and a bristle of a moustache. At the end of the service, the man vanished into thin air. They tried to trace him. They wondered if a prying journalist or prankster might have been impersonating Hitler, but the boatman, Neil MacGillivary, swore that nobody had crossed the water to Inch Kenneth. Was it a ghost?

In 1944, a stray German bomber dropped its load close enough for the blast to break Unity's bedroom window.

'You can thank Uncle Adolf for that!' said Jessica, who was visiting at the time.

Bobo would get up to all sorts of silliness in those years and with the Campbells her father often despaired of what a naughty little brat she was and how she didn't listen to anybody. Mary came to assume her former role, but even she couldn't keep Unity out of trouble all the time.

Bobo decided that she would make a cake, so she mixed together fifty or sixty eggs, without any flour (this at a time when food was strictly rationed).

She liked to go out rowing a lot with Mary, just the two of them. How else would she spend her time? Reading, singing, painting, sewing. Lord Redesdale, too, enjoyed painting woodwork. Unity preferred painting on canvas or drawing on paper. Bobo was never bored; she always kept herself occupied, even if it was just a walk around the island.

The British government was convinced that she was a very dangerous woman. But on a remote island she was treated like a poor soul, sincerely accepted among the locals. They didn't judge her.

Nevertheless, the outlandish stories and damning rumours about her never ceased, many of them false – for example, that she was in the habit of flashing midnight signals to German submarines using her bicycle lamp. In any event, no subs appeared.

What *was* true was that Unity was seen boarding a rowboat to head across to mainland Mull for an evening of dance with Neil the boatman.

'My, you are a big strapping woman,' said Neil flirtingly as Unity hopped aboard.

She laughed at his remark. 'I'm strong too. Would you like me to row?'

Despite being a tall and clumsy, slightly brain-damaged woman, Unity put her mind to it and danced very well that night. She was in a great mood.

'I think you Scottish people are frightfully lucky for being able to wear the kilt,' she said to Neil with a wink as they waltzed and reeled together.

The other people there were friendly to her and it turned out to be an exceptionally fun night that she would never forget.

The Second World War ended the following year, with the German army, navy, and air force soundly defeated, virtually annihilated, having been forced by Hitler to fight to the bitter end. Many Nazi soldiers preferred to die rather than surrender. Hitler had married Eva Braun in his bunker in Berlin, where he and his commanders were hiding out from the bombs. Not long after the exchange of wedding vows, when there were no longer any illusions and it was clear that all was lost, Hitler and Eva Braun went into a room together and never came out again. A gunshot rang out, and a cyanide pill was swallowed. It was a double suicide.

Great displays of rejoicing and festivity followed the end of the war, and a multitude of people all over Europe and beyond took to the streets to kiss Allied soldiers, throw flowers at victorious tanks, and cheer and weep with joy, hoping to usher in a new era of optimism and peace. But Unity wasn't rejoicing. She felt horrible; she could only see the downside of what the war had wrought. Not only was it death and destruction on an unprecedented scale – so many millions dead, so many millions of Reichsmarks of damage done, so many precious things destroyed forever – but just as devastatingly to her, it was the death of her illusions, the death of her ideals, the death of her idol.

In the spring of 1948, Unity's health took a turn for the worse.

Her illness began as a chill, followed by throbbing headache and nauseous vomiting. Doses of sulphathiazole were administered for several days and there was subsequently a marked improvement in her condition and no more vomiting, although she continued to suffered from a fever.

Unity was at times quite delirious, once mumbling, 'I made such a mess of my life... Such an unfortunate mess.' This was as close to a verbal denial of Hitler and Nazism as she was capable of; it was all the world would have.

Shortly after that, she stopped speaking.

One day she was rushed to the nearest hospital, and arrived in fairly good shape at midnight to be given penicillin. She was examined by a surgeon named Dr Crawford, who determined that there was cerebral swelling around the bullet lodged in her brain. He then got in touch with a brain specialist, and they agreed to move her to the latter's brain unit for emergency attention. But from that instant her condition deteriorated very fast, and it was decided that she should not be moved. Unity's pupils dilated, and she sank into a violent epileptiform seizure, which was followed by calm Cheyne-Stokes respiration, and then, within a few minutes, death.

Unity Mitford died on 28 May 1948 at 9.50 p.m. On the death certificate, the cause of death was written as 'Purulent Meningitis, Old Gun-shot Wound'.

She had planned her funeral and handpicked the hymns. Samuel Barber's *Adagio for Strings* was played. There wasn't a dry eye.

Everyone had abandoned Unity in those years leading up to the Second World War. And nobody could stand her in those final years when she was brought back on a stretcher as Hitler's fanatical little friend. Only her best friend Mary, the English girl who had constantly been with her in Munich, had stayed on with her – to the detriment of her own reputation. Unity's devotion to Hitler had destroyed her life and cost her almost all her friends. Hitlerism fucked her up, and had a destructive influence on her whole life. She lived to regret it – what an error of judgment, what a waste. But by then it was too late. Little did people know or realise that she had renounced and repented. Mankind would not forgive her, but would a loving and forgiving God? Thanks to Mary's intervention, Unity retrieved her old copies of the anti-Semitic *Der Stürmer*, her gold party badge, her autographed copy of *Mein Kampf*, the portrait. She threw it all in the trash at Inch Kenneth. At first, she had been keeping the items and found it hard to believe that Hitler caused the Holocaust, insisting that it was propaganda. It was excruciating for her to think anything about Hitler besides good things. But at last she believed it. She could no longer deceive herself and deny his monstrous evil. She awoke to the reality of the genocidal massacre, to the objective truth of its injustice. It all sank in. It was an incalculably disastrous revelation for her, absolutely crushing.

After Unity's death, her father acted as if she was still at the mansion, as if her presence on the island could still be felt. He was on his way to Iona with the family one time when he changed his mind and turned back because he felt certain that Bobo was stranded outside the front door, waiting to be let in. He heard strange noises too, which he believed were Unity. He would mournfully sigh and mutter about his precious Bobo, over and over: 'How sad it all was... How sad it all is...'

The doctors had given her ten years to live, and she died within eight.

Lord Redesdale kindly gave Unity's writing desk to Mary as a gift, in gratitude for her friendship to his daughter.

'Keep it in memory of Unity,' he said.

'Thank you, sir.'

It was antique Edwardian and quite large, well-crafted and made of mahogany, with various decorative wood inlays and five drawers on both sides.

He couldn't stop thinking and talking about his Unity. He would spend winters at High Wycombe or London and summers on Inch Kenneth. There would be picnics and everyone in the Mitford clan would come up to the little island retreat.

It was quite a gathering when they all assembled under the same roof or sky – communists, fascists and conservatives – such a clash of personalities, temperaments and views. And always, very near, the invisible presence of Unity hung over all, like a haunting shadow or pungent scent in the brisk sea air.

Afterword

This is a true story of the people and events surrounding the life of Unity Mitford, a free-spirited and rebellious British girl who fell in love with Hitler at the height of his power and overwhelming diabolical charm in Germany. Wherever possible, personalities, events and dialogues are accurately reconstructed and represented – in the case of dialogue, often taken *verbatim* from archival sources and interviews. It is based largely on the recorded reminiscences of the people who knew Unity. The photographs in the book are reproduced from my own private collection. Just like the novel *Schindler's Ark*, from which the film *Schindler's List* was made, this book is based in fact. Written in the method of creative, or narrative, non-fiction, it is what I call my 'non-fiction novel.'

I was asked by one of my literary colleagues, while discussing the writing of this book, the following question: 'How could such an ugly heart lurk under such a beautiful face?' I explained that Unity Mitford certainly wasn't the only well-known case of a pretty young girl whose outer beauty stood as a contrast to her inner ugliness. Take, for example, the case of Irma Grese, who was the youngest Nazi to be convicted and executed after the Second World War. Just twenty-two years of age, she had been dubbed 'The Beautiful Beast' for her good looks and the sadistic excesses that she engaged in at the concentration camp Bergen-Belsen, where she had begun as a camp guard and quickly moved to the top of the ranks as senior supervisor. After the liberation of the camp by British Allied Forces, she was tried and found guilty of crimes against humanity for torturing and murdering Jewish inmates. Yet, on the outside, she looked like a beautiful angel.

But to compare Unity to Irma and call her simply an evil monster and leave it at that would be a gross simplification. The full and complete portrait of who Unity really was isn't so black and white. It's shades of grey. Yes, she made many bad choices, but there's more to this unusual girl if one digs deeper into her life, as I have done in trying to understand her and what exactly happened to her and how. Very, very few people are completely good. The vast majority of us are a complex composite of flattering and not-so-flattering traits. The difference is, the better among us try to express the good in themselves and suppress the bad. No one is perfect; the best we can each do as individuals is to try to become better people in our lives. Unfortunately, Unity gave no thought to this, and her lifestyle became consumed by a racist, fascist ideology. But, as I say, very few people are completely bad. Apart from her ideology, she was a normal girl. She lived and laughed and cried like a normal girl, with normal hopes and goals and dreams. She was capable of kindness and good humour. She wasn't some three-headed monster spewing fire. It's quite possible, and perhaps likely, that her interest in and support of Mosleyism and Hitlerism would have waned or disappeared altogether, had she lived beyond the 1940s. Indeed, in her final years she seemed to have almost forgotten about Hitler, and her former passion for fascism/Nazism was replaced by a religious one.

I make no apology for Unity Mitford or her fascist and Nazi anti-Semitism, which can only be called evil and regrettable. This book has simply been an attempt to tell her story as objectively and as interestingly as I was able to in a compelling storytelling narrative style (whereas non-narrative can be confined to just the dry facts and figures). And there can be no doubt, regardless of one's personal opinion of Unity, that her life story is fascinating and that she is a fascinating figure. I also hope that this book serves as a lesson about how a vulnerable, young and nonconformist mind can be brainwashed by hateful doctrine and how this can damage and even destroy a person. By her example, Unity ultimately proved herself to be both perpetrator and victim. And that, perhaps, is the saddest thing of all.

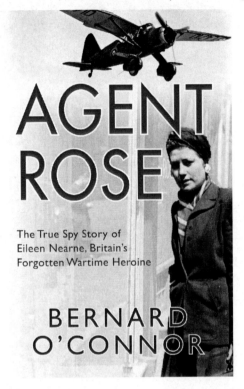